The Beginners Prayer Book

"Praying the Alphabet to God"

Calvin L. McCullough Sr.

WESTBOW
PRESS®
A DIVISION OF THOMAS NELSON
& ZONDERVAN

WestBow Press books may be ordered through booksellers or by contacting:

WestBow Press
A Division of Thomas Nelson & Zondervan
1663 Liberty Drive
Bloomington, IN 47403
www.westbowpress.com
844-714-3454

ISBN: 978-1-6642-4599-0 (sc)
ISBN: 978-1-6642-4600-3 (hc)
ISBN: 978-1-6642-4598-3 (e)

Library of Congress Control Number: 2021919940

Print information available on the last page.

WestBow Press rev. date: 10/07/2021

Table of Contents

Great Prayer Quotes

"Prayer is the idea of wishing for something from the depth of our hearts and bringing that desire forward to the throne of God." — Greg Laurie,

"True prayer is a way of life, not just for use in cases of emergency. Make it a habit, and when the need arises you will be in practice." — Billy Graham

"Listening is the beginning of prayer, and what we listen to is the voice of God, God that cannot deceive or be deceived. In the silence of the heart God speaks; let God fill us, then only we speak." — Mother Teresa

"Our prayers may be awkward. Our attempts may be feeble. But since the power of prayer is in the one who hears it and not in the one who says it, our prayers do make a difference." — Max Lucado

"I have been driven many times upon my knees by the overwhelming conviction that I had no where else to go. My own wisdom and that of all about me seemed insufficient for that day." — Abraham Lincoln

"True prayer is a way of life, not just for use in cases of emergency. Make it a habit, and when the need arises you will be in practice." — Billy Graham

"Prayer lays hold of God's plan and becomes the link between his will and its accomplishment on earth. Amazing things happen, and we are given the privilege of being the channels of the Holy Spirit's prayer." — Elisabeth Elliot

"To be a Christian without prayer is no more possible than to be alive without breathing." — Martin Luther

"True prayer is neither a mere mental exercise nor a vocal performance. It is far deeper than that - it is spiritual transaction with the Creator of Heaven and Earth." — Charles Spurgeon

"I know that the Lord is always on the side of the right; but it is my constant anxiety and prayer that I and this nation may be on the Lord's side." — Abraham Lincoln

"Prayer makes a godly man, and puts within him the mind of Christ, the mind of humility, of self-surrender, of service, of pity, and of prayer. If we really pray, we will become more like God, or else we will quit praying." — E.M. Bounds

"We are precious to God . . . He is waiting for you to come to Him in prayer. He wants to honor you by filling you with His presence." — Mother Teresa

"To be a Christian without prayer is no more possible than to be alive without breathing." — Martin Luther

"God shapes the world by prayer. The more praying there is in the world the better the world will be, the mightier the forces against evil." — "The goal of prayer is the ear of God." — E.M. Bounds

"It is not enough to say the prayers, you have to pray the prayers; pray with your heart and mind." — Mother Teresa

Dedication

"This Book is Dedicated to our Lord Jesus Christ, the true teacher and the perfecter of our Faith and Holiness!" Jesus, we thank You for your love, mercy, peace and grace. We thank You, Jesus, for the blood You shed so we may share in Your righteousness and gain a right relationship with God the Father through You.

This Book is Also Dedicated to my Wife:
Claudia P. McCullough

Introduction

Have you ever tried to pray, and found your mind wandering and couldn't keep focus? Or have you ever tried to pray for an hour and could not? I have tried so hard to focus when praying, but more often than not my mind drifts, and I must pull myself back to the area that I was supposed to be praying about. Sometimes it can be hard to concentrate on prayer.

Well, this Book is a tool to help you concentrate and focus when there are so many distractions!

Prayer is an important part of everyone's life, because the Bible tells us that as surely as we live, says the Lord, 'every knee will bow before me; every tongue will confess to God' (Romans 14:11 NIV). This means that every person that has ever walked the face of the earth will come before a Holy God with their head bowed and on their knees with a prayer of confession.

For the Christian, this prayer is the "Sinners Prayer." It is my opinion, based on Proverbs 15:29, that once a person gets to the age of accountability and they have not made Jesus their Lord and Savior, the first prayer God/Jesus hears from that person is the "Sinners Prayer."

If you have never made Jesus the Christ your Lord and Savior, I invite you to pray this simple prayer with me:

> *Father God, I know that I have broken your laws and my sins have separated me from you. I am truly sorry. And now I want to turn away from my past sinful life, and turn toward you. Please forgive me, and help me avoid sinning again. I believe that your son Jesus Christ died for my sins, He was resurrected from the dead, I believe He is alive and hears my prayer. I invite you, Jesus, to become the Lord of my life, to rule and reign in my heart from this day forward. Now please send your Holy Spirit to help me*

to obey you and to do your will for the rest of my life.
In Jesus' name, I pray, Amen."

In every religion, we find that pray and/or meditation is a part of life. I have found that the Bible tells us that the answer to everything (problems, requests, guidance or direction) in our lives is prayer mixed with faith which is described as our divine and uniquely powerful weapon. The Bible is also the testimony that God hears the cries of his children and answers them as a loving Father. Proverbs 15:29 states, "The LORD is far from the wicked but he hears the prayer of the righteous."

But what is Prayer? And why should I pray and how do I pray?

1. The answer to the first question, what is prayer:
    *   Prayer is simply communication with God/Jesus. It is telling Him the secrets and the concerns of our hearts.

2. The answer to the second question, why should I pray:
    *   Because prayer was important to Jesus, and prayer should be equally important to us.
    *   We should pray because it is important to be able to listen and hear from God.
    *   It is because of the salvation God the Father has given us. Through the blood of His Son Jesus, we have access to God the Father.
    *   If we neglect praying, we neglect God, the salvation He gave us, and the access He has given us into eternal life through the blood of Jesus.

3. The answer to the third question, how do I pray:
    *   Begin your prayer by saying who you are praying to: "Heavenly Father, God the Creator, or Lord God."
    *   Second, praise and thank God for the specific things in your life (tell Him how much you love Him and how much you adore Him).

- Third, ask God to forgive you for all your sins you have done this day (name each sin you know you have committed).
- Fourth, express your needs and your desires and ask that they be fulfilled according to His will (GOD's). Ask Him for His guidance and protection, for wisdom and discernment.
- Then close by saying "in the Name of Jesus!"

To enhance our communication with God, here are some basic things we should remember to do as a part of our A-B-C prayer!

First, is "**A**", we should "**A**SK," in Jesus' name. Jesus tells us in the Bible to ask in His name when we pray to the Father (John 14:13-14; 15:16; 16:23-24, 26 NIV). However, we must pray in line and according to God's will!

The second is "**B**", to receive anything from God we must "**B**ELIEVE" in Jesus. This means we must have Faith in God/Jesus, because Hebrews 11:6 states, "And without faith it is impossible to please God, because anyone who comes to him must believe that he exists and that he rewards those who earnestly seek him."

And third, is "**C**", is "**C**ONFESS." We are to confess our sins to God and to others that we have sinned against and be reconciled with God/Jesus. First John 1:9 tells us, "If we confess our sins, he is faithful and just and will forgive us our sins and purify us from all unrighteousness."

As you spend time praying through these prayers that the Holy Spirit has allowed me to write, please meditate on what you have just read "Out Loud." Ask God/Jesus to allow your mind, body, and soul to become one with the Holy Spirit.

Here are Ten more Reasons why we should pray the ABC's of Scriptures.

1. Praying Scripture helps us memorize the Word of God and the promises of God.
2. Praying Scripture helps us keep our focus on the goodness of God.
3. Praying Scripture teaches us biblical doctrine.

4. Praying Scripture helps us to develop a better relationship with God the Father, His Son Jesus Christ, and the Holy Spirit.
5. Praying Scripture helps us grow in our faith.
6. Praying Scripture helps us express appreciation and gratitude to God the Father, His Son Jesus Christ, and the Holy Spirit.
7. Praying Scripture teaches us to trust God in every situation in life.
8. Praying Scripture helps us to avoid temptation and find direction and strength.
9. Praying Scripture helps us to receive the perfect answers.
10. Praying Scripture glorifies God the Father.

As Christians, we must understand that prayer is an important part of every Christian's life. However, one of the problems we have had with praying is focus. I mean having one's own mind, heart, spirit, and soul on one accord. The Bible tells us, "We do not know what we ought to pray for, but the Spirit himself intercedes for us with groans that words cannot express" (Romans 8:26 NIV). Therefore, using this book can help you concentrate and focus in a practical way when praying!

This book can be a 21st Century Psalm Book for you.

How to Pray the Alphabets . . .

It is simple. Starting with the letter "A," pray through all the attributes of God (who He is) by using biblical and or scriptural words. Next, pray through all the adoration you have for God using the letter "A" (the things He has done). The third area for prayer is your requests using the letter "A". The fourth area of prayer is for all the people you know whose name begins with that letter "A". Then, proceed through the alphabet, praying for all four areas per letter.

> Note: It will also be important to use biblical and/ or scriptural words for a number of reasons; we should pray them because it glorifies God the Father, because Jesus prayed this way, and because it will help you focus on what is most important.

I have broken each letter into four separate sections so we can focus on one letter and area at a time, to keep us from jumping all over the place. The first area will be worship, the second is praise, the third area is your personal requests, and the fourth area will be for the people in our lives.

First, Worship:
> We worship God because of who He is: He is Elohim, the first name used of God in the Bible to designate Him (Genesis 1:1). This name means Strong and Mighty One. He is Adonai, which means "Master," "Ruler" or "Lord" (Genesis 15:1-2). He is Jehovah, which is His personal name, meaning redeemer, and it is His covenant name.

Second, Praise:
> We praise God because of the things He has done. God has delivered us out of darkness into His marvelous, wonderful light (1 Peter 2:9 NIV), through His Son Jesus Christ. Jesus has saved us from God's wrath

and the penalty of sin and death, and He has given us eternal life. Therefore, we are to praise God for His works in creation, His providence, His redemption, and for our salvation.

Third, Our Personal Requests:
The Bible states in John 16:24, "Until now you have not asked for anything in my name. Ask and you will receive, and your joy will be complete." Also, in John 14:13 Jesus said, "And I will do whatever you ask in my name, so that the Son may bring glory to the Father."

Fourth, for the People in Our Lives:
First and foremost, we must pray for salvation in every individual life. James tells us: "Therefore confess your sins to each other and pray for each other so that you may be healed. And the prayer of a righteous man is powerful and effective" (James 5:16 NIV). Matthew tells us to "Love your enemies and pray for those who persecute us" (Matthew 5:44 NIV). Paul tells us in Ephesians, "And pray in the Spirit on all occasions with all kinds of prayers and requests. With this in mind, be alert and always keep on praying for all the saints" (Ephesians 6:18 NIV).

I found that it was easier for me after I used this format that I am sharing with you. I have added Bible verses with each line to line-up our prayers with the Word of God. Also, there is a blank work sheet behind each alphabet section for you to create your own alphabet prayer.

So, let's get started!!!

A

Worship God because of who He is:

- Lord God you are *Adonai*, my "Master," "my Ruler" and "my Lord" – Ex. 6:31; 1 Kg. 4:26
- I cry, "*Abba*, Father" because I have received the Spirit of son-ship – Gal. 4:6; Mk. 14:36; Rom. 8:15
- I ask you *almighty* God, please keep me from the evil one – Gen. 17:1; 2 Sam 7:27; Rev, 11:17
- You are my *anointed* High Priest that lives forever – Heb. 3:1; 4:14; 10:12
- Jesus, you are the *Author* and Perfecter of my faith – Heb. 12:2
- You are also the *Author* of Life – Acts 3:15
- You are the *Alpha* and Omega – Rev. 1:8; Rev. 22:13
- Father God you are *amazing* in *all* your *acts* – Isa. 29:14
- Jesus has been my *advocate* before the Father – 1 John 2:1; Job 16:19; John 14:26;
- I worship you for the *advent* (His coming) – Rev. 22:11-12; 3:11;
- Jesus, you are my *all* in *all* – Philip. 3:8; Col. 1:17
- You are the *Ancient* of Days – Dan. 7:9, 13, 22
- Father God you are the final *authority* of everything – Deut. 4:2; Matt. 24:35;
- Jesus, you are the *apostle* of God's Procession – Heb. 3:1
- Lord God you are simply *awesome*!!! – Deut. 10:17; Ps. 68:35

Praise God for what he has done:

- I praise you, Jesus, for Your *atoning* Blood – Rom. 3:25; Heb. 9:13-14
- Lord, I stand in *awe* of *all* you have done – Ps. 33:8; Isa. 66:2
- God, I thank you for your *agape* love you have extended – John 3:16; Rom. 5:8
- I thank you for *answering* my prayers – Matt. 5:45; Jam. 1:17

- Your *acts are always* for my good and your glory – Philip.2:13; Matt. 5:16
- Lord your *armor* protects me 24/7 – Eph. 6:10-15
- Your *affliction* for me is forever – Ps. 34:17-20
- Your Word tell me that I *am* the *apple* of your eyes – Psalm 17:8; Deut. 32:10; Ps. 17:8
- Lord God, I *adore* you for all the mercy and grace you have shown me - Ps.27:13; 145:9
- Father, you give me an *abundance* of love and peace through Jesus Christ – Eph. 3:20
- Lord, your ears are *attentive* to my prayers when I pray – 2 Chron. 7:15; Neh. 1:11; Psalm 130:2
- Father God, I *acknowledge* that you are the creator of everything – Rev. 4:11; Col.1:16
- Lord Jesus, I thank you for the *angels* you encamp around me – Ps. 34:7
- Lord Jesus, I am *accepted* in you alone – Rom. 15:7
- I praise you, Lord, because you *adopted* me *as* your very own child – Col. 1:12-13; Gal. 4:5
- You have *always* loved me – Ps. 136:2; 1 John 4:7, 19.
- I praise you for the *assistance* I receive from you every minute of my life – John 10:29
- I praise you for the *abilities* and gifts you have given me – 1 Cor. 14:1; 1 Cor. 12:4-6
- I thank you, Lord, for the books of *Amos* and the book of *Acts* that teaches me your Word – *Amos; Acts*

Prayer Requests:

- Please *alter* my character to look more like you, Jesus – Col. 3:10; Eph. 5:1-2
- Father, thank you for *abiding* in me, so I can *Abide* in you – John 15:7
- Father God, I *abound* in the love you have for me – 1 Tim. 1:14; 1 Thess. 3:12
- Jesus, help me to be ready for your *appearance* – 1 Pet 1:13
- Jesus, *anchor* me in THE FAITH – Heb. 6:19
- Lord, I pray that you *abstain* me – 2 Tim. 2:19

- And help me to *avoid* every form of sin – Prov. 4:15; 2 Tim. 2:16
- Let everything that is an *abomination* to you, be an *abomination* to me – Lev. 20; Ez. 16:20
- Father God, please keep your *arms* of protection around me – Ps. 89:13; Isa. 52:10
- Lord Jesus, help me to be a faithful *ambassador* for *Abba* – Eph. 6:2;
- Father God, your love, grace, and mercy are so *attractive* to me – Prov. 2:10
- Lord Jesus, I truly *apologize* and repent to you for *all* my sins – 1 Sam. 15:25; Ps. 25:11
- Lord, please encamp your *angels all around* me – Ps. 34:7; Luke 4:10; Heb. 1:14
- Now, *according* to your Word, I can reign with You – Ps. 116:65, 133

Prayer for the People in your Circle:

- Lord I pray for my *adversaries*, that they may be truly blessed. I pray for the *athletes* that are under my care. I pray for all who have the gift of *administrator*.
- I pray for *Anthony*, that he will know you, God, more intimately and glorify you in every area of his life (Pray for any specific needs you know about).
- I pray for *April*, that she will know you, God, more intimately and glorify you in every area of her life (Pray for any specific needs you know about).
- I pray for *Antonio*, that he will know you, God, more intimately and glorify you in every area of his life (Pray for any specific needs you know about).
- I pray for *Annette*, that she will know you, God, more intimately and glorify you in every area of her life (Pray for any specific needs you know about).

A

Worship God because of who He is:

- _____
- _____
- _____
- _____
- _____
- _____
- _____
- _____
- _____
- _____
- _____
- _____
- _____
- _____

Praise God for what he has done:

- _____
- _____
- _____
- _____
- _____
- _____
- _____
- _____
- _____
- _____
- _____
- _____
- _____
- _____

Prayer Requests:

- _____
- _____
- _____
- _____
- _____
- _____
- _____
- _____
- _____

Prayer for the People in your Circle:

- _____
- _____
- _____
- _____
- _____
- _____
- _____
- _____
- _____

B

Worship God because of who He is:

- Jesus, you are the *Bread* of Life – John 6:35; John 6:48
- You are the *Bright* Morning Star – Rev. 22:16
- Jesus, you are the *Branch* of Righteousness – Jer. 33:15; 23:5
- You are the only one that *blesses* – Gen. 49:25; Deut. 15:6
- Tell me that I'm the *beloved* of you God, Father - Colossians 3:12; Deut. 33:12
- Lord Jesus you are the most important stone in the *building* – Eph. 2:20
- Jesus, you are the *Brazen* serpent in the *book* of Numbers – Num. 21:8-9
- Father you are the Lord my *Banner* (*Jehovah-Nissi*) – Ex. 17:15; Isa. 49:22
- Jesus, you are the *Beginning* and the End – Rev. 22:13
- Father God, you are the one to *behold, because* you will make everything new – Rev. 21:5; Isa. 43:19

Praise God for what He has done:

- Lord God, walk *before* me and *beside* me to show me your perfect way. – Prov. 14:2
- I am Holy and without *blame before* you – Eph.1:4; 1 Thess. 5:23
- Lord, your *Belt* of Truth keeps me from the lies of Satan – Eph. 6:14
- I praise you for all the *benefits* I have in you – Ps. 68:19; Gal. 5:1
- God, all the works of your hands are *beautiful* – Eccl. 3:11
- Jesus, I thank you for the *breath* of life – Gen. 2:7; Lam. 4:20
- I am grateful for the *blood* you shed for me – 1 John 5:6; Heb. 9:12, 22.
- Lord, I thank you for the *banquet* you have prepared for me – Isa. 25:6; Rev. 19:9

- Thank you for *baptizing* me in the name of Jesus, washing away my sins – Acts 2:38
- Lord Jesus, when you return, the *brilliance* of your glory will *bring* joy to all the saints – Rev. 1:16; Ez. 10:4
- I praise you *because* I'm free from the *bondage* of Satan, sin, and the law – Gal. 5:1
- Jesus, you are the *Beloved* Son – 1 John 5:1; Gal. 4:7
- I thank you for giving me your *book* (the *Bible*, your Holy Word) – John 17:17; Ps. 119:16
- Jesus, I thank you for *bearing* my sins on the cross at Calvary – 1 Pet. 2:24
- I praise you, Lord, *because* You have made me a part of your *body* – Rom. 12:5

Prayer Requests:

- Lord God, please *build* me into a spiritual house you alone may dwell – Rom. 8:9
- Let *brotherly* love flow from my heart everyday – 2 Pet. 1:7; Rom. 12:10
- Lord Jesus, please remove all *bitterness* from my heart and replace it with Your love – Eph. 4:31;
- Father God, keep me prepared for the coming of the *Bridegroom* – Matt. 25:10
- Jesus, I truly *believe* you died and rose again just for me – Rom. 4:25, 7:4
- Father God, thank you that I have *been born* again and have received salvation – 1 Pet. 1:3, 23.
- Please keep me inside the *boundaries* you have set for all of mankind – Ps. 74:17; 2 Cor. 10:13
- Lord, please *bless* all of my *brothers* – Ps. 66:8; Gen. 28:3
- Jesus, may everything I say and do *be biblical* – Col. 3:17;
- Lord Jesus, I love you from the *bottom* of my heart – Eph. 6:4; Ps. 116:1

- Father God, please fight all of my *battles* – Ex. 14:14; Deut. 20:4;
- LORD, please be close to me when I'm *brokenhearted* and when my spirit is crushed, and *bind* up my wounds – Ps. 34:18; 147:3

Prayer for the People in your Circle:

- I pray for the *bereaved* Families, God, that your love would comfort them, and please give them Your peace that passes all understanding. I pray that every *bride* would be obedient to the Word of God. I pray that the *bus* drivers would keep our children safe.
- I pray for *Bobby*, that he will know you, God, more intimately and glorify you in every area of his life (Pray for any specific needs you know about).
- I pray for *Brenda*, that she will know you, God, more intimately and glorify you in every area of her life (Pray for any specific needs you know about).
- I pray for *Bryant*, that he will know you, God, more intimately and glorify you in every area of his life (Pray for any specific needs you know about).
- I pray for *Brittney*, that she will know you, God, more intimately and glorify you in every area of her life (Pray for any specific needs you know about).

B

Worship God because of who He is:

- _____
- _____
- _____
- _____
- _____
- _____
- _____
- _____
- _____
- _____
- _____
- _____
- _____
- _____
- _____

Praise God for what he has done:

- _____
- _____
- _____
- _____
- _____
- _____
- _____
- _____
- _____
- _____
- _____
- _____
- _____
- _____
- _____

Prayer Requests:

- _____
- _____
- _____
- _____
- _____
- _____
- _____
- _____
- _____
- _____

Prayer for the People in your Circle:

- _____
- _____
- _____
- _____
- _____
- _____
- _____
- _____
- _____
- _____

C

Worship God because of who He is:

- Lord God, you *created* all things, and by Your will they exist and were *Created* – Rev. 4:11; Col.1:16; John 1:3
- Lord, you are my *comforter* – Isa. 51:12; Jer. 8:18
- Father God, you are a *Consuming* fire – Heb. 12:28
- God, you are a Father that never stops *caring* for your *children* – Ps. 23:1; Matt. 10:30-31
- You are the *covenant* keeping God – Deut. 7:9
- Jesus, you are the *Chief Cornerstone* (Eph. 2:20) and *Capstone* – Acts 4:11; 1 Pet. 2:7
- You are the *Chief* Shepherd (1 Pet. 5:4)
- Jesus, you are The *Christ*, the Anointed One and the Messiah – Matt. 16:16; Acts 17:3
- Lord God, you are the God of all *comfort* – 2 Cor. 1:3-4;
- You are the *Captain* of the Lord's host – Joshua 5:13-15
- You are the wonderful *Counselor* – Isa. 9:6
- Father, you are a faithful and *Compassionate* God – Ps. 116:5; 2 Cor. 1:3
- Lord God, nothing or no one *can compare* to you – Isa. 40:18; Ps. 40:5

Praise God for what he has done:

- *Christ* Jesus, I love you for your sweet *communion* (fellowship) with me – Lk. 22:18-20
- Jesus, I am *complete* in you, and I'm a *child* of God's - 1 Pet. 1:23
- Through you, Jesus, I am more than a *conqueror* – Rom. 8:37
- Lord, I am Free from *condemnation* because of the *Cross* of Jesus – Rom, 5:16, 18
- Thank you for sending me the *Counselor* (Holy Spirit) – John 14:16
- Lord Jesus, I *can* do all things through You – Phil. 4:13
- Thank you for *courage* and strength today – Joshua 1:9

- I praise you, Lord, because I'm *chosen* in God – 1 Thess. 1:4
- Jesus, I thank you for guaranteeing the *covenant* you have with me – Heb. 7:22
- Thank you for the Incorruptible *Crown* (1 Cor. 9:25), the *Crown* of Rejoicing (1 Thess. 2:19-20), the *Crown* of Life (Jam. 1:12), the *Crown* of Glory (1 Pet. 5:2-4), and the *Crown* of Righteousness you have waiting on me (2 Tim. 4:8).
- I thank you for giving me your *Canon*, your Holy Word (the Bible) - John 1:1; Ps. 119:16
- Lord God, please set me apart through your *consecration* – Rom. 6:16, 12:1
- Father God, I praise you for *creation*; for bringing everything into existence – Heb. 11:3
- Jesus, I thank you for bearing my sins on the *Cross* at *Calvary* and dying for me through the *crucifixion* of that *cross* – Heb. 2:17; 1 John 4:10
- Jesus, I will *call* your name first in times of *crisis* – Ps. 50:15; Rom. 10:13
- Thank you for *clothing* me in your righteousness – Job 29:14; Isa. 61:10; Rom. 13:14
- Lord God, my heart is truly *content* with you – Matt. 6:25-26, 33; Heb. 13:5
- I thank you, Lord, for the books of 1 & 2 *Chronicles*, 1 & 2 *Corinthians* and the book of *Colossians* that teach me your Word – 1 & 2 Ch.; 1 & 2 Cor.; Col.

Prayer Requests:

- Jesus, please keep my *children* safe in this sinful world – Ps. 5:11
- Lord God, *cross-examine* my mind and heart and *change* them to be like Jesus – Rom. 12:2
- Give me *compassion* for those in my *circle* of influence – Ps. 103:4, 13
- Lord, *create* in me a *clean* heart – Ps. 51:10
- *Cleanse* me from all unrighteousness – 1 John 1:9; Ps. 51:2
- Father, please develop in me the *characteristics* of Jesus – Phil. 1:6

- *Consecrate* me, Lord Jesus, and set me aside for your glory – Rom. 6:16, 12:1
- Allow me to be the *Church* you are looking for – Eph. 5:27
- Lord, help me to obey your *commands* – Ps. 119:60; 166.
- Help me to *conform* to your will, O Lord (Rom. 12:2), and *consume* me with your Spirit (Acts 2:28)
- Father God, I pray that when people *call* my name, that they might *call* me *Christian* or *Christ*-like – 1 Cor. 11:1; Acts 11:26
- Lord Jesus, help me to keep my heart *circumscribed* from this world – Ezek. 36:26; Deut. 30:6
- Lord, I pray for the *conversion* for the lost people in my family – Mk. 16:16; Jam. 4:8
- Jesus, please let me walk *close* by your side – Ps. 23:4; Job 16:27
- Lord God, help me face all of life's *challenges* successfully – Jam. 1:2-4
- Father God, please keep my spouse and me *connected* with your love – 1 Cor. 13:4-8
- Jesus, give me the *confidence* to operate in faith – 2 Thess. 3:4
- Lord Jesus, I praise you because you are *concerned* about me – Phil. 4:10

Prayer for the People in your Circle:

- I pray for my *church* and the *churches* around the world; I pray for my *co-workers*. I pray for the people that have the gift of Biblical *counseling*.
- I pray for *Clinton,* that he will know you, God, more intimately and glorify you in every area of his life (Pray for any specific needs you know about).
- I pray for *Claudia,* that she will know you, God, more intimately and glorify you in every area of her life (Pray for any specific needs you know about).

- I pray for *Cymee'*, that he will know you God more intimately and glorify you in every area of his life (Pray for any specific needs you know about).
- I pray for *Cymone*, that she will know you God, more intimately and glorify you in every area of her life (Pray for any specific needs you know about).

C

Worship God because of who He is:

- _____
- _____
- _____
- _____
- _____
- _____
- _____
- _____
- _____
- _____
- _____
- _____
- _____
- _____
- _____

Praise God for what he has done:

- _____
- _____
- _____
- _____
- _____
- _____
- _____
- _____
- _____
- _____
- _____
- _____
- _____
- _____
- _____

Prayer Requests:

- _____
- _____
- _____
- _____
- _____
- _____
- _____
- _____
- _____
- _____

Prayer for the People in your Circle:

- _____
- _____
- _____
- _____
- _____
- _____
- _____
- _____
- _____
- _____

D

Worship God because of who He is:

- Father God, you are the purest form of *Deity* — Col. 2:9
- Lord God, your commands are *delightful* to my soul – Mal. 3:12; Ps. 119:172
- Jesus, you are the *door* to eternal life – John 10:9
- Lord, you are *divine* in your love, your mercy, and your grace – 2 Pet. 1:3; Rom. 1:20
- Father God, no words can never *describe* who you are – Isa. 40:28-29; Num. 23:19
- Jesus, you are the *deliverer* of all mankind – Isa. 49:26
- You are my *doctor* in times of sickness - (*Jehovah-ROPHE*: "The Lord Who Heals") Ex. 15:22-26.
- Jesus, you are *dependable* in every situation of life – Heb. 13:5; Deut. 31:8; Josh. 1:5

Praise God for what he has done:

- I am *delivered* from the power of *darkness* and translated into God's kingdom of light – Col. 1:13; Eph. 6:12
- I thank you for *dying* on the cross for my sins – 1 Pet. 2:24; 1 Pet. 3:18
- Thank you for *disciplining* me, Lord Jesus– Col. 1:16, Gat. 5:25
- Lord Jesus, I thank you for *dealing* with me as your child – Rom. 8:14
- All your commands are *delightful* to your servant – Ps. 119:16, 35, 47
- Lord, I take *delight* in you . . . you alone give me the *desires* of my heart – Ps. 37:4
- Father God, all of your *decrees* are just and for my good – 2 Sam. 22:23; Ps. 119:16
- Jesus, I *dedicate* my life to you, because you gave your life for me – Rom. 12:1; Col. 3:17

- I praise you for paying the *debt* I could not pay – 1 Cor. 6:20; 1 Tim. 2:6
- Jesus, you are the center of my *devotion* – Ps. 138:1; 1 Chron. 29:20
- Lord Jesus, you never *disappoint* me at any time – Heb. 13:5
- Jesus, you *demonstrated* True Love at the cross – Rom. 5:8
- Father God, you have kept me *day* after *day* in your grace – 2 John 1:3
- I Praise you, LORD, for your *dominion* (ownership) and all your works – Ps. 103:22
- I thank you, Lord, for the books of *Deuteronomy* and the book of *Daniel* that teach me your Word – Deut.; Dan.

Prayer Requests:

- Jesus, please *develop* in me a *determination* to pursue You always – Matt. 6:33
- Lord, continue to *direct* me in your ways – Ps. 25:4-5
- Lord, may your *desires* be my *desires* – Ps. 38:9
- Father God, please help me to be a *devout* person in all my ways – Acts 10:2
- Lord, I pray that my *doctrine* of the Gospel never strays from your truth – 2 John 1:9
- Father God, I come to You to *dedicate* my life to You, today – 1 Sam. 1:28
- Lord God, never allow the word *divorce* to be in my home – Matt. 19:8
- Jesus, I pray that each time I open your Word I *discover* something new – Ps. 119:18
- God, please keep my *daughters* safe – Ps. 12:7
- Father, please *deposit* in me the characteristic of Jesus – Eph. 1:14
- Jesus, please give me your *discernment* in all things – Phil. 1:9-10; 1 John 4:1

Prayer for the People in your Circle:

- I pray for Knowledge and wisdom for my *doctors, dentist,* and everyone with that title of *director.*
- I pray that *Dennis* will know you, God, more intimately and glorify you in every area of his life (Pray for any specific needs you know about).
- I pray for *Denise,* that she will know you, God, more intimately and glorify you in every area of her life (Pray for any specific needs you know about).
- I pray for *Dewayne,* that he will know you, God, more intimately and glorify you in every area of his life (Pray for any specific needs you know about).
- I pray for *Diana,* that she will know you, God, more intimately and glorify you in every area of her life (Pray for any specific needs you know about).

D

Worship God because of who He is:

- _____
- _____
- _____
- _____
- _____
- _____
- _____
- _____
- _____
- _____
- _____
- _____
- _____
- _____

Praise God for what he has done:

- _____
- _____
- _____
- _____
- _____
- _____
- _____
- _____
- _____
- _____
- _____
- _____
- _____
- _____

Prayer Requests:

- _____
- _____
- _____
- _____
- _____
- _____
- _____
- _____
- _____
- _____

Prayer for the People in your Circle:

- _____
- _____
- _____
- _____
- _____
- _____
- _____
- _____
- _____
- _____

E

Worship God because of who He is:

- God, you are *Elohim* (the Strong and Mighty One) – Zeph. 3:17
- Lord, you are *El-Shaddai* (the God Almighty) – Gen. 49:24
- Lord, you are *El-Elyon* (the Strongest Strong One) – Ps. 57:2
- Lord, you are *El-Roi* (the Strong one who Sees) – Isa. 28:2
- Lord, you are *El-Olam* (the *Everlasting* God) – Isa. 40:28
- Father God, you are *Elijah*, "my God is LORD" – Ps. 140:6; Dan. 9:4; John 20:28
- Lord, your Word *encourages* me *every* day – Isa. 41:10; John 14:27
- Lord God, you are The One *Eternal* God – Deut. 33:27
- God, all *exaltation* belongs to you alone – Ps. 97:9
- Jesus, how *excellent* is you name – Ps. 8:9
- You are the *Everlasting* Father - Isa. 9:6
- You are the *ever*-present God – Ps. 46:1
- Father God, there is no god *equal* to you in any way – Phil. 2:7
- You are the only God to be *edified* – Acts 20:32

Praise God for what he has done:

- Lord, you *envelop* me with your love, mercy, and your grace – Eph. 1:23
- Father God, your Word says I'm *established* to the end in and through Christ Jesus – Col. 2:7
- Because of your love, I can *endure* the race set before me – Heb. 12:1
- I thank you for *enduring* the cross and hostility for my sins – Heb. 12:2
- I thank you, Jesus, for *encamping* your angels around me – Ps. 34:7
- I thank you, Lord, for the *everlasting* love you have for me, your servant – Jer. 31:3
- Jesus, thank you for the gift of *eternal* life – Rom. 6:23

- I praise you because I am the *elect* of God through your blood, Jesus – Eph. 1:7; 1 Pet. 1:2
- Lord, I thank you for *every* blessing I have received – 1 Chr. 16:34; Num. 6:24
- Jesus, your blessing is *exceeding* all my *expectations* – Ps. 145:15-16
- Thank you, Holy Spirit, for *entering* into my heart – Ps. 51:10; Gal. 4:6
- I praise you, Lord, for the *edification* – Eph. 4:11-12
- Lord, your Word is *encouraging* to my heart and soul – Ps. 119:28
- I thank you, Lord, for the books of *Exodus, Ezra, Esther, Ecclesiastes, Ezekiel,* and the book of *Ephesians* that teach me your Word – Ex.; Ez.; Est.; Eccl.; Ezek.; Eph.

Prayer Requests:

- Lord God, please keep my *eyes* on Jesus, and never let them stray – Heb. 12:2
- Help me, Jesus, with the *edification* of your people – Eph. 4:12
- Teach and guide me as I *evangelize* the lost – Acts 1:8
- Jesus, help me love my *enemies* – Lk. 6:27; Mk. 11:24
- Father God, please let me *experience* your power, glory, and your joy – Ps. 143:8
- Lord, please *engage* and *encourage* me through your Holy Spirit – Isa. 40:29
- Jesus, teach me and guide me in *evangelism* – Rom. 1:16
- Father, please *enhance* my discernment in all things – Phil. 1:9
- Lord, help me to be *effective* for the name of Jesus – Phil. 1:6
- Father, help me to Except my calling and responsibilities – Ezra 10:4

Prayer the People in your Circle:

- Lord Jesus I pray for the *elders* in my church. Lord, give them Your wisdom to lead Your people. I pray for the *electricians* and the *engineers* that you will keep them safe.

- I pray that *Edward* will know you, God, more intimately and glorify you in every area of his life (Pray for any specific needs you know about).
- I pray for *Elizabeth*, that she will know you, God, more intimately and glorify you in every area of her life (Pray for any specific needs you know about).
- I pray for *Emmanuel*, that he will know you, God, more intimately and glorify you in every area of his life (Pray for any specific needs you know about).
- I pray for *Ebony*, that she will know you, God, more intimately and glorify you in every area of her life (Pray for any specific needs you know about).

E

Worship God because of who He is:

- _____
- _____
- _____
- _____
- _____
- _____
- _____
- _____
- _____
- _____
- _____
- _____
- _____
- _____
- _____

Praise God for what he has done:

- _____
- _____
- _____
- _____
- _____
- _____
- _____
- _____
- _____
- _____
- _____
- _____
- _____
- _____
- _____

Prayer Requests:

- _____
- _____
- _____
- _____
- _____
- _____
- _____
- _____
- _____
- _____
- _____

Prayer for the People in your Circle:

- _____
- _____
- _____
- _____
- _____
- _____
- _____
- _____
- _____
- _____

F

Worship God because of who He is:

- Lord, you are a *Faithful* God – Lam. 3:22-23; Deut. 7:9; 1 Thess. 5:24
- You are a *Forgiving* God – Isa. 34:25
- God, you are the *Father* of all Righteous – 1 John 2:1; John 17:25
- Lord Jesus, you are a *friend* in times of need – John 15:15
- God, you are my *fortress* in times of trouble – Ps. 46:1
- Jesus, you are the *firstborn* of all creation, the *first fruit,* and you are the *first* to rise from the dead – Col. 1:15; 1 Cor. 15:20-23; Rev. 1:5
- *Father* God, you are the *fountain* of life that never run dry – Ps. 36:9
- Lord Jesus, you are my solid *foundation* that will never move – 1 Cor. 3:11

Praise God for what he has done:

- , and established in the *faith* through Jesus – Col. 2:7
- Lord, you are the one that *fights* all my battles – Ex. 14:14; Deut. 20:4
- I thank you *for* all the *Fruit* of the Spirit that lives inside of me – Gal. 5:22-23
- Jesus, thank you *for forgiving* my sins – Eph. 1:7; Heb. 9:14
- Lord, you have prepared a *feast for* me at your table – Ps. 23:5; Rev. 19:6-9
- I praise you because I'm set *free* – John 8:31-33
- Jesus, I praise you because you *foreordained* my salvation – 1 Pet. 1:20; Rom. 8:29
- Because of you, Jesus, I have *favor* with the *Father* – Ps. 90:17; Prov. 3:4
- Jesus, I praise you because I have a bright *future* with you – Heb. 9:11, 10:1; Rom. 8:17
- Your hands, O Lord, made me and *formed* me – Ps. 119:73

Prayer Requests:

- Lord, please remove anything *fake* in me, and help me to be a good *friend* to others – Ps. 1:1-2
- *Father*, please allow my *fellowship* with others to be as the *fellowship* You have with Your Son Jesus – John 17:20-26
- Lord Jesus, help me *fulfill* the commitments I have made – Pro. 16:3
- Jesus, keep me *focused* and operating in your will – Col. 3:2; Heb. 12:2
- Lord God, please *form* me into the image of your son Jesus – Rom. 8:29
- *Father* God, *fill* me with your Spirit – Rom. 15:3
- Lord, please *fix* the broken hearted – Ps. 147:3

Prayer for the People in your Circle:

- I pray that my entire *family* may know You as Lord and Savior, and give their lives to you today as Your servants. I pray for all of the *first* responders. I pray for all of the *farmers* around the world.
- I pray that *Fred* will know you God more intimately and glorify you in every area of his life (Pray for any specific needs you know about).
- I pray for *Francis*, that she will know you, God, more intimately and glorify you in every area of her life (Pray for any specific needs you know about).
- I pray for *Frank*, that he will know you, God, more intimately and glorify you in every area of his life (Pray for any specific needs you know about).
- I pray for *Felicia*, that she will know you, God, more intimately and glorify you in every area of her life (Pray for any specific needs you know about).

F

Worship God because of who He is:

- _____
- _____
- _____
- _____
- _____
- _____
- _____
- _____
- _____
- _____
- _____
- _____
- _____
- _____
- _____

Praise God for what he has done:

- _____
- _____
- _____
- _____
- _____
- _____
- _____
- _____
- _____
- _____
- _____
- _____
- _____
- _____
- _____

Prayer Requests:

- _____
- _____
- _____
- _____
- _____
- _____
- _____
- _____
- _____
- _____

Prayer for the People in your Circle:

- _____
- _____
- _____
- _____
- _____
- _____
- _____
- _____
- _____
- _____

G

Worship God because of who He is:

- *God,* you are my *Gracious* Father – Ps. 145:8
- You are Jehovah, you are the one true *GOD* – Jer. 10:10
- Lord Jesus, you are my *Great* High Priest – Ps. 110:4; Heb. 6:20
- Jesus, you are the *gate* I must go through – John 10:9
- You are the *Good* Shepherd – Ps. 23:1; 1 Pet. 5:4; John 10:11
- Lord, you are the King of *Glory* – Ps. 24:8-10
- You are the *Great* I AM – Ex. 3:14; John 8:58; John 15:5; John:14-6

Praise God for what he has done:

- Lord, I love your *glory* . . . Lord show me your *glory* – John 17:24; Rev. 15:8
- Thank you for the *gifts* you have *given* me – 1 Pet. 4:10
- Lord *God,* I know every *good* and perfect *gift* comes from you, Father – Jam. 1:17; 1 Cor. 12:4
- I thank you for the *grace* you *give* me every day – 1 Cor. 1:4; Eph. 1:7
- Thank you for *giving* me eternal life – John. 3:16; 1 John 2:25
- Lord Jesus, you have been so, so *good* to me – Ps. 13:6
- Jesus, when I think of all the blessing you have *given* me, my heart is filled with *gratitude* – Ps. 28:7
- Father *God,* I thank you for the day when I will share in Your *glory* and receive *glorification* – Rom. 8:17; 2 Thess. 1:10
- Lord, when you have tested me, help me to come forth as pure *gold* – Job 23:10
- Lord, your faithfulness continues through all *generations* – Ps. 100:5
- I thank you, Lord, for the books of *Genesis* and the book of *Galatians* that teach me your Word – Gen.; Gal.
- I praise You because *greater* is the Holy Spirit that is within my, than he that is in the world – 1 John 4:4

Prayer Requests:

- Teach me through your *grace*, Lord, so that Your *grace* will be my first response – 2 Tim. 2:1
- Holy Spirit, help me when I share the *gospel* with others – Matt. 24:14
- *God,* will you *glorify* me as Jesus requested in John chapter 17 – John 17:20-24
- Father *God*, please *give* me the strength to make it through this race – Phil. 4:13
- Lord, I pray that Your *goodness* and mercy will follow me all the days of my life – Ps. 23:6
- Holy Spirit, please *give* me *guidance* when darkness surrounds me – Romans 2:19

Prayer for the People in your Circle:

- I pray for the *governor* of each State; that he/she would do Your Will, Lord!
- I pray that you will bless my *grandparents* with good health, and keep them safe. I pray for all of our military *generals*, and the men and women that work in auto *garages*.
- I pray that *Greg* will know you, God, more intimately and *glorify* you in every area of his life (Pray for any specific needs you know about).
- I pray for *Gwen*, that she will know you, God, more intimately and *glorify* you in every area of her life (Pray for any specific needs you know about).
- I pray for *Gary*, that he will know you, God, more intimately and *glorify* you in every area of his life (Pray for any specific needs you know about).
- I pray for *Gail*, that she will know you, God, more intimately and *glorify* you in every area of her life (Pray for any specific needs you know about).

G

Worship God because of who He is:

- _____
- _____
- _____
- _____
- _____
- _____
- _____
- _____
- _____
- _____
- _____
- _____
- _____
- _____
- _____

Praise God for what he has done:

- _____
- _____
- _____
- _____
- _____
- _____
- _____
- _____
- _____
- _____
- _____
- _____
- _____
- _____

Prayer Requests:

- _____
- _____
- _____
- _____
- _____
- _____
- _____
- _____
- _____
- _____

Prayer for the People in your Circle:

- _____
- _____
- _____
- _____
- _____
- _____
- _____
- _____
- _____
- _____

H

Worship God because of who He is:

- Lord, you are *HOLY, HOLY, HOLY!!!* – 1 Pet. 1:16; Isa. 6:3; Rev. 4:8
- I will forever say *Hallowed* is your name – Matt. 6:9; Ex. 20:11
- Jesus, you are the *High* Priest that lives forever – Heb. 6:20
- You are the Lord of *heaven* and earth – Isa. 47:16
- Jesus, you are the *Head* of the church, and *Head* of my life – Col. 1:18; 1 Cor. 11:3
- Lord God, I say *hallelujah* to your *Holy* name, for salvation and glory and power belong to you alone – Ps.145:21
- I *honor* you, God, because you are Jehovah – Rev. 4:11
- Lord, you are the God That's *Healer* (Jehovah-Rophe) – Ex. 15:26
- Father God, you are the Lord of *Hosts* (Jehovah-Sabaoth) – 1 Sam. 1:3
- You are the *High* and Mighty God – Ps. 93:4; Rev. 1:8

Praise God for what he has done:

- Jesus, you *have* made it possible for me to enter the *Holy* of *Holies* – 2 Cor. 3:16-17
- Lord Jesus, I will walk *humbly* before you – Mic. 6:8
- Father, I have been *healed* by the stripes of Jesus from all my afflictions – Isa. 53:5
- Your Word tells me I am the *head* and not the tail – Deut. 28:13
- I thank you for the *hope* I *have* in you, Lord Jesus – Ps. 31:24; Jer.29:11
- I thank you for sending the *Holy* Spirit – John 14:26
- I thank you for *hearing* me when I pray – Ps. 65:2; Ps. 34:15
- I thank you; I *have* a *home* in *heaven*, not made by *human hands* – 2 Cor. 5:1
- Lord, your *helmet* of Salvation keeps my mind free from the evil one – Eph. 6:17

- Lord, I say *Hosanna* to your name because you are the true savior – Mk. 11:10; 1 Cor. 6:20
- All *honor* and respect belong to you, O LORD – Ps. 86:9; 1 Cor. 6:20
- There is nothing too *hard* for You, God! – Gen. 18:14; Job 42:2; Jer. 32:17, 27
- I thank you, Lord, for the books of *Hosea, Habakkuk, Haggai,* and the book of *Hebrews* that teach me your Word – Hos.; Hab.; Hag.; Heb.
- Lord God, you *have* raised up a *horn* of salvation for Your people – Lk. 1:69

Prayer Request:

- Lord, keep my *heart* from growing *hard* or bitter – Ps. 51:10; Eph. 3:17-18
- Cleanse me with *hyssop,* and I will be clean; wash me, and I will be white as snow – Ps. 51:7
- Fill me with your *Holiness,* Lord – Rom. 15:13; Eph. 3:19
- *Help* me, Jesus, to *hate* what is evil and cling to what is good – Rom. 12:9; Ps. 97:10
- *Help* me to live *honorably* in every way, before you and the world; and may I never live as a *hypocrite* – 1 Pet. 2:12; Matt. 6:5
- Father God, *help* me to keep a *hymn* on my lips and a song of praise in my *heart* – Ps. 40:3; Eph. 5:19
- Lord God, let me *hear* your voice every time you call me – Heb. 3:7; Ps. 85:8
- Lord, please build upon me; and let not gates of *hell* prevail over me – Matt. 16:18
- Lord, please put a *hedge* of protection around me to keep me safe from Lucifer - Job 1:10

Prayer for the People in your Circle:

- I pray for everyone that I know that is *hospitalized;* I ask that you would *heal* their minds, bodies, and souls. I pray for all the *health* Care workers, and *human* Services workers.

- I pray that *Henry* will know you, God, more intimately and glorify you in every area of his life (Pray for any specific needs you know about).
- I pray for *Hannah*, that she will know you, God, more intimately and glorify you in every area of her life (Pray for any specific needs you know about).
- I pray for *Hunter*, so he will know you, God, more intimately and glorify you in every area of his life (Pray for any specific needs you know about).
- I pray for *Harriett*, that she will know you God more intimately and glorify you in every area of her life (Pray for any specific needs you know about).

H

Worship God because of who He is:

- _____
- _____
- _____
- _____
- _____
- _____
- _____
- _____
- _____
- _____
- _____
- _____
- _____
- _____

Praise God for what he has done:

- _____
- _____
- _____
- _____
- _____
- _____
- _____
- _____
- _____
- _____
- _____
- _____
- _____
- _____

Prayer Requests:

- _____
- _____
- _____
- _____
- _____
- _____
- _____
- _____
- _____
- _____

Prayer for the People in your Circle:

- _____
- _____
- _____
- _____
- _____
- _____
- _____
- _____
- _____
- _____

I

Worship God because of who He is:

- Father, you are the great "*I* AM" – Ex. 3:14; John 8:58
- Jesus, you are *Immanuel* (God with us) – Isa. 7:14
- You are the LORD of *Israel* – Ps. 135:4
- Father God, your presence *in* all creation is *immanent* (about to happen) – Col. 1:17
- *I* worship you, Jesus, because of your act of *incarnation* (becoming human) – John 1:14; Heb. 2:17; John 1:1-3
- God, you are *incomprehensible* (not able to be understood) – Ps. 145:3; Rom. 11:33
- Lord, to know all of you *is inconceivable* (not capable of being imagined or grasped) – Ps. 145:3; Rom. 11:33
- Father God, you are *incredible in* all that you do for me – Isa. 55:9; Ps. 147:5

Praise God for what he has done:

- Lord God, thank you for making me *in* your *image*, and *I'm* being changed into the *image* of your Son, Jesus – 2 Cor. 3:18; Rom. 8:29
- *I* thank you, Jesus, for *interceding* on my behalf – Rom. 8:34; Heb. 7:25
- *I'm* your child, *I* am born again of the *incorruptible* seed by you Word, God – 1 Pet. 1:4; 1 Cor. 9:25
- Lord, you make the *impossible*, possible for me – Luke 18:27; Heb. 7:25
- *I* praise you, Lord, for the *inheritance I* have through you Jesus – Col. 1:12; Gal. 3:29
- Thank you, Lord, that all you have for me *is imperishable* – 1 Pet. 1:23
- Father God, your Word is *irresistible* to my soul – Ps. 119:103, 105
- *I* have justification because of the *imputation* of your righteousness, Jesus – 1 Cor. 1:30; Rom. 1:17

- Lord, *I* thank you for the times you used me as your *instrument* to speak to your people – John 15:16
- *I* thank you, Lord, that *I'm invited* to the "Wedding Feast of the Lamb" – Rev. 19:9
- Lord God, your Word *is inerrant, infallible,* and *inspired* TRUTH – 2 Sam. 22:31; Ps. 12:6
- Jesus, *I* thank you that one day *I* will be *in immortality* with you – 1 Cor. 15:54
- *I* thank you, Lord, for the book of *Isaiah* that teaches me your Word – Isa.
- Lord God, thanks be to You for Your *indescribable* gift – 2 Cor. 9:15

Prayer Requests:

- Lord, *increase* my love for others – 1 Thess. 3:12; Rom. 12:10
- Jesus, please wash away all my *iniquities* – Ps. 51:2; 1 John. 1:9
- Lord, keep me from all and every *immoral* way – 1 Cor. 6:18; 1 Cor. 6:9
- Give me a godly *integrity,* Lord – Prov. 20:7; 2 Cor. 7:2
- Lord, keep the *inscription* of your Word on my heart – Ps. 119:11; Prov. 7:3
- *Increase* me with your wisdom and knowledge – Prov. 9:11; Eph. 1:17
- Father God, let me *invoke* your name first – Ps. 55:16; Ps. 91:15
- God, never allow me to act *inappropriate* before you – Ps. 69:6; Prov. 30:9
- And keep me from becoming an *idolator* – 1 John 5:21; 1 Thess. 1:9
- Lord Jesus, help me to be a better *influence* for your living Word – Phil. 4:8-9; Matt. 5:13-14

Prayer the People in your Circle:

- Lord Jesus, *I* pray for the *individuals* I work with on my Job, Church and House. *I* pray for the *industrial* works that make the things we need. *I* pray for the people that have the gift of *instructor.*

- I pray that *Isaiah* will know you, God, more intimately and glorify you in every area of his life (Pray for any specific needs you know about).
- I pray for *Iris,* that she will know you, God, more intimately and glorify you in every area of her life (Pray for any specific needs you know about).
- I pray for *Israel,* so he will know you, God, more intimately and glorify you in every area of his life (Pray for any specific needs you know about).
- I pray for *Ivory,* that she will know you, God, more intimately and glorify you in every area of her life (Pray for any specific needs you know about).

I

Worship God because of who He is:

- _____
- _____
- _____
- _____
- _____
- _____
- _____
- _____
- _____
- _____
- _____
- _____
- _____
- _____

Praise God for what he has done:

- _____
- _____
- _____
- _____
- _____
- _____
- _____
- _____
- _____
- _____
- _____
- _____
- _____
- _____

Prayer Requests:

- _____
- _____
- _____
- _____
- _____
- _____
- _____
- _____
- _____
- _____

Prayer for the People in your Circle:

- _____
- _____
- _____
- _____
- _____
- _____
- _____
- _____
- _____
- _____

J

Worship God because of who He is:

- You are *Jehovah,* my Lord God and redeemer – Ps. 18:2; Job 19:25
- LORD, you are *Jehovah-Jireh* (you're my provider) – Gen. 22:14; Phil. 4:19
- *Jesus,* you are the LORD of LORDS and KING of KINGS – Rev. 17:14
- *Jesus,* you are the Righteous *Judge* of all mankind – John 5:22
- Father God, you are a *Jealous* God – Ex. 20:5; Deut. 4:24
- God, you are a *just* God – 2 Thess. 1:6; Heb. 6:10
- *Jesus,* you were the King of the *Jews,* and now King forever – Matt. 27:11
- *Jesus,* you are the Lion of the tribe of *Judah* – Rev. 5:5
- *Jesus,* you are our Wonderful Counselor, our Mighty God, the Eternal Father, and Prince of Peace – Isaiah 9:6
- *Jesus,* your name is the sweetest name I know – Phil. 1:29; Jer. 10:6

Praise God for what he has done:

- Lord, I am never alone, because you are on every *journey* with me– Isa. 41:10; Deut. 31:6
- I thank you, *Jesus,* that I am a *joint* heir with you – Rom. 8:17
- *Jesus,* you are the same yesterday, today and forever – Heb. 13:8
- Lord *Jesus,* you have brought *justice* to your servant – Heb. 10:30; Eccl. 3:17
- *Jesus,* your righteousness has imputed *justification* unto me – 1 Cor. 1:30
- Lord *Jesus,* you have given me *joy* that the world cannot take away – John 14:27
- I am *justified* and freed by Your grace, Christ *Jesus* – Rom. 3:24

- Lord, I will make a *joyful* noise unto You, LORD – Ps. 100:1
- I thank you, Lord, for the books of *Joshua, Judges, Job, Jeremiah, Joel, Jonah, James, Jude* and the four books of *John* that teach me your Word – Jos.; Jdg.; Job; Jer.; Joel; Jon.; Jam.; Jude; 1, 2, 3 John

Prayer Request:

- *Jesus*, you teach me how to be ready for your *judgment* – 2 Cor. 5:10; Heb. 9:27
- Lord *Jesus*, help me to reflect you on my *job* – Matt. 5:13-14, 16
- Lord *Jesus*, let me *join* you in the sky when you return – 1 Thess. 4:17; 1 Cor. 15:51-54
- Lord God, let me live in the New *Jerusalem* which is spoken of in Revelation – Rev. 3:12; Rev. 21:2

Prayer the People in your Circle:

- I pray for the *janitors* in my workplace because they give me a picture of a servant heart. I ask you to bless them as they serve others. I also pray for *judges* of our courts, that they demonstrate your *justice* in-line with your will.
- I pray that *Joshua* will know you, God, more intimately and glorify you in every area of his life (Pray for any specific needs you know about).
- I pray for *Joy*, that she will know you, God, more intimately and glorify you in every area of her life (Pray for any specific needs you know about).
- I pray for *James*, so he will know you, God, more intimately and glorify you in every area of his life (Pray for any specific needs you know about).
- I pray for *Jessica*, that she will know you, God, more intimately and glorify you in every area of her life (Pray for any specific needs you know about).

J

Worship God because of who He is:

- _____
- _____
- _____
- _____
- _____
- _____
- _____
- _____
- _____
- _____
- _____
- _____
- _____
- _____
- _____

Praise God for what he has done:

- _____
- _____
- _____
- _____
- _____
- _____
- _____
- _____
- _____
- _____
- _____
- _____
- _____
- _____
- _____

Prayer Requests:

- _____
- _____
- _____
- _____
- _____
- _____
- _____
- _____
- _____
- _____

Prayer for the People in your Circle:

- _____
- _____
- _____
- _____
- _____
- _____
- _____
- _____
- _____
- _____

K

Worship God because of who He is:

- Jesus, you are *King* of *Kings* and Lord of All – 1 Tim. 6:15; Rev. 19:16
- You are the *King* of Israel – John 1:49
- You are the *King* of the Jews – Matt. 27:11
- You are the *King* of the Nations – Rev. 15:3
- Lord, your *Kingdom* can never be shaken – Ps. 21:7; Ps.112:6;
- God, you are the *kind* Father of all creation – Col. 1:15-16
- Lord Jesus, you are my *Kinsman*-redeemer – Gal. 3:13
- Jesus, you are my *kind* Savior – Isa. 43:11
- Jesus, you are the *keeper* of my Soul – Ps. 121:5
- You are the Eternal *King* – 1 Tim. 1:17

Praise God for what he has done:

- Lord, I praise you for the loving *kindness* you have shown me – Ps. 63:3; Ps. 36:7
- Jesus, you have given me the *keys* to loosen and bind here on earth – Matt. 16:19
- Father God, you alone have *kept* the enemy away from me – Ps. 59:1; Ps. 44:7
- Father God, I *kneel* before you because you are GOD – Eph. 3:14; Ps. 95:6
- I thank you, Lord, for the books of 1 & 2 *Kings* that teach me your Word – 1 & 2 Ki.
- Jesus, I praise you because you stand at my door *knocking*, you let me hear Your voice, and You have come in to continually eat with me – Rev. 3:20
- I praise you for Psalm 95:6, that I can come bow down and *kneel* before you, LORD our Maker, and worship in freedom – Ps. 95:6

Prayer Request:

- Lord, please *keep* your arms around me – Ps. 3:3; Ps. 16:32
- My desire is to *know* you intimately, Lord – Eph. 3:19; Eph. 1:17
- Jesus, let your *kindness* be my calling card to others – Pro. 17:17
- Lord Jesus, I pray for *Knowledge* and wisdom – Ps. 111:10; Pro. 9:10
- Lord, may your Word *keep kindling* in my heart – Ps. 119:11; Col. 3:16
- Jesus, *keep* me from *killing* people with my tongue – Ps. 141:3; Ps. 39:1
- Lord, *kiss* me with your lips: for Your love is better than wine – Song 1:2
- Jesus, you have told me to ask and it will be given to me; seek and I will find; to *knock* and You will open the door for me – Luke 11:9; Matt. 7:7

Prayer the People in your Circle:

- I pray for the *Kinsman*-redeemers of the world that keep their responsibility to their relatives. I pray for everyone that works in a *kitchen.*
- I pray that *Kevin* will know you, God, more intimately and glorify you in every area of his life (Pray for any specific needs you know about).
- I pray for *Kate*, that she will know you, God, more intimately and glorify you in every area of her life (Pray for any specific needs you know about).
- I pray for *Ken*, so he will know you, God, more intimately and glorify you in every area of his life (Pray for any specific needs you know about).
- I pray for *Karen*, that she will know you, God, more intimately and glorify you in every area of her life (Pray for any specific needs you know about).

K

Worship God because of who He is:

- _____
- _____
- _____
- _____
- _____
- _____
- _____
- _____
- _____
- _____
- _____
- _____
- _____
- _____
- _____

Praise God for what he has done:

- _____
- _____
- _____
- _____
- _____
- _____
- _____
- _____
- _____
- _____
- _____
- _____
- _____
- _____
- _____

Prayer Requests:

- _____
- _____
- _____
- _____
- _____
- _____
- _____
- _____
- _____
- _____

Prayer for the People in your Circle:

- _____
- _____
- _____
- _____
- _____
- _____
- _____
- _____
- _____
- _____

L

Worship God because of who He is:

- Father God you are *Love* – John 3:16; 1 John 3:1; Rom. 5:8; Eph. 2:4-5
- You are *LORD* [YHWH] (Jehovah) our Righteousness – Jer. 23:6
- Jesus, you are the *Light* of the World – John 8:12
- *Lord* Jesus, you are the *Lion* of Judah – Rev. 5:5
- You are the *Lord* of *Lords* – Rev. 19:16
- Jesus, you are the *Lamb* of God that has taken away all my sins – John 1:29
- You are the *Lamb* without blemish – 1 Pet. 1:19
- *Lord* Jesus, you are the *Living* bread of *Life* – John 6:51
- Father God, you are *LORD* of all creation – Col. 1:15-16
- You are the *Last* Adam, a *life*-giving spirit – 1 Cor. 15:45
- Jesus, you are the *Lord* of Glory – 1 Cor. 2:8
- You are the *Lord* of All – Acts 10:36
- *LORD*, you are *longsuffering*, filled with great mercy, and have forgiven my iniquity and transgression – Num. 14:18
- *Lord* You are the Rose of Sharon, and the *Lily* of the Valley – SS. 2:1
- Jesus, you are the *Living* Word of *Life* – John 1:1

Praise God for what he has done:

- God, I thank you for you *loved* me so much you gave your Son – Zep. 3:17; 1 John 3:1; John 3:16
- *Lord* your *loving*-kindness endures forever – Ps. 100:5; Ps. 136:1
- Thank you, Father, for *lavishing* me with your *love* – 1 John 3:1
- I am confident that I will see your *love* and goodness in the *land* of the *living* – Ps. 27:13
- Jesus, thank you for showing me the way, the truth, and the *life* – John 14:6
- Father God, your Word is a *lamp* for my feet – Ps. 119:105

- Jesus, thank you for redeeming me from the penalty of the *law* – Eph. 1:7; Gal. 3:13
- I thank you, Lord, for the books of *Leviticus*, *Lamentations*, and the book of *Luke* that teach me your Word – Lv.; Lam.; Lk.

Prayer Request:

- Jesus, please give me that *Living* Water – John 4:14; John 7:38-39
- Father God, I ask that you would *lay* your hand on me – Ps. 139:5, 10
- Holy Spirit, please *lead* me into all righteousness – Ps. 5:8; Ps. 27:11
- Father God, *look* into my heart and remove all the ungodliness – Ps. 51:10
- Jesus, I'm asking you to *lighten* my *load* when I'm burdened – Ps. 55:22; Matt. 11:29-30
- *Lord*, please put a hedge of protection around me to keep me safe from *Lucifer* - Job 1:10
- *Lord* Jesus, please *listen* to me when I pray – Ps. 143:1; Ps. 5:3

Prayer for the People in your Circle:

- *Lord* I pray for the *leaders* of the *land* in which we *live*. I pray for the *leader* of my small group. I pray for the *laboratory* technicians to be kept safe, and for the *librarians* that assist people.
- I pray that *Logan* will know you, God, more intimately and glorify you in every area of his life (Pray for any specific needs you know about).
- I pray for *Linda*, that she will know you, God, more intimately and glorify you in every area of her life (Pray for any specific needs you know about).

- I pray for *Lindsay,* so he will know you, God, more intimately and glorify you in every area of his life (Pray for any specific needs you know about).
- I pray for *Lisa,* that she will know you, God, more intimately and glorify you in every area of her life (Pray for any specific needs you know about).

L

Worship God because of who He is:

- _____
- _____
- _____
- _____
- _____
- _____
- _____
- _____
- _____
- _____
- _____
- _____
- _____
- _____

Praise God for what he has done:

- _____
- _____
- _____
- _____
- _____
- _____
- _____
- _____
- _____
- _____
- _____
- _____
- _____
- _____

Prayer Requests:

- _____
- _____
- _____
- _____
- _____
- _____
- _____
- _____
- _____
- _____

Prayer for the People in your Circle:

- _____
- _____
- _____
- _____
- _____
- _____
- _____
- _____
- _____
- _____

M

Worship God because of who He is:

- Lord God, you are Jehovah-*M'Kaddesh* (you're *my* sanctifier) – Lev. 20:7-8
- Lord Jesus, you are the *Majestic* One – Jude 1:25
- Jesus, you are the Great *Mediator* of the New Covenant – Heb. 9:15
- Jesus, you are the one and only True *Messiah* – John 17:3
- You are the High Priest in the order of *Melchizedek* – Heb. 7:17
- Father God, you are *Magnificent* in everything you do – Ps. 145:3
- You are the *marvelous maker* of all things – Ps. 118:23
- You are *Master*, Lord and King – John 13:13; 1 Tim. 6:15
- Jesus, you are the bright *Morning* Star – Isa. 9:6
- Jehovah, you have sent your *messenger* to us – Jud. 6:22; 1 Chron. 21:15; Zech. 1:12
- You are the *Mighty* God – Isa. 9:6; Josh. 22:22
- Lord, my God, how *majestic* is your name in all the earth – Ps. 8:9

Praise God for what he has done:

- Jesus, you have delivered *me* of darkness and placed *me* in your *marvelous* and wonderful light – 1 Pet. 2:9
- I thank you for your *mercy* – Heb. 4:16; Ps. 51:1
- Lord God, you have put your Law (Word) in *my mind* and heart – Jer. 31:33; Heb. 10:16
- Jesus, I praise you for *my* greatest *miracle*; You changed *my* life from a dead person unto a living person – Rom. 6:11; Eph. 2:5
- Lord, I thank you for your comfort when I'm in *mourning* – Eph. 2:5

- I thank you, Lord, for the books of *Micah, Malachi, Matthew,* and the book of *Mark* that teach me your Word – Mic.; Mal.; Matt.; Mk.
- Lord, we praise you for the *many* blessing you have given us – Phil. 4:19; Jam. 1:17

Prayer Request:

- Father, help *me* to keep *my motives* pure when I pray – Pro. 4:23; Ps. 121:7
- Lord, be *merciful* when I go astray, and bring *me* back – Heb. 5:2
- Father, forgive *me* when I *make mistakes* along the way – 1 John 1:9
- Lord God, allow the *manifestation* of Your Spirit *move* in *my* life – Rom. 8:9
- Lord Jesus, I pray that *my marriage might* be pleasing to you – Ps. 19:14
- Father God, I pray that you will help *me* to be faithful in the *missions* you have assigned *me* – Acts 1:8; Matt. 28:19-20
- Lord, I pray that You will help *me* to always rule over *money,* and that *money* will never rule over *me* – Deut. 15:6; Luke 12:15
- Jesus, help *me* to grow *mature* in *memorizing* your Word – Jer. 20:9
- Father, also help *me* to attain the whole *measure* of the faith and knowledge of your Son Christ Jesus in which *mankind* can understand – Rom. 12:3
- Lord, I need YOU every *minute* of *my* life – Ps. 16:2; Ps. 25:5

Prayer for the People in your Circle:

- I pray for all the *ministers* that they *might* lead your people in your truth. And I also pray for all the *missionaries* all around the world. I also pray for the *mechanics* that keep us *moving.*
- I pray for the *mayor* of each City, that he/she would do Your Will!

- I pray that *Michael* will know you, God, more intimately and glorify you in every area of his life (Pray for any specific needs you know about).
- I pray for *Michelle*, that she will know you, God, more intimately and glorify you in every area of her life (Pray for any specific needs you know about).
- I pray for *Matthew*, so he will know you, God, more intimately and glorify you in every area of his life (Pray for any specific needs you know about).
- I pray for *Mary*, that she will know you God more intimately and glorify you in every area of her life (Pray for any specific needs you know about).

M

Worship God because of who He is:

- _____
- _____
- _____
- _____
- _____
- _____
- _____
- _____
- _____
- _____
- _____
- _____
- _____
- _____
- _____

Praise God for what he has done:

- _____
- _____
- _____
- _____
- _____
- _____
- _____
- _____
- _____
- _____
- _____
- _____
- _____
- _____
- _____

Prayer Requests:

- _____
- _____
- _____
- _____
- _____
- _____
- _____
- _____
- _____
- _____

Prayer for the People in your Circle:

- _____
- _____
- _____
- _____
- _____
- _____
- _____
- _____
- _____
- _____

N

Worship God because of who He is:

- Lord, you are my Jehovah-*Nissi* (you're my banner of victory) – Ex. 17:15
- Father God, there is *nothing negative* about you – Eccl. 7:14
- LORD GOD, the creator of the world; Your eternal power and divine *nature* have been clearly seen - Rom. 1:20
- *Nothing* is too hard for you, LORD GOD - Gen. 18:14; Job 42:2; Jer. 32:17
- Jesus, you are the only Prophet from *Nazareth* in Galilee - Matt. 21:11
- Lord God, you are the "Pillar of Fire" that guides by *night* to give me a light - Ex. 13:21

Praise God for what he has done:

- Jesus, I praise you because you have *never* left me or forsaken me – Deut. 31:8; Heb. 13:5
- Thank you, Jesus, for the *new* life and *new* birth I have in You – 2 Cor. 5:17; Rom. 6:4
- Father, your Spirit *nurtures* my soul – 1 Thess. 5:23
- I love you, Lord, because you have *never* failed me – Psalm 136
- Lord, your mercies are *new* every morning – Lam. 3:22-23
- All *nature* worships you, Jesus, the seas, sky, and land – Ps. 66:4; Rev. 5:13
- I praise you, Lord, because your love can *never* grow cold for me – 1 John 4:10, 19
- I am a *new* creature through Your blood – 2 Cor. 5:17
- I praise you because I'm *no* longer ruled by the forces of evil, but by You – Rom. 6:14; Rom. 8:9
- Jesus, you gave your body to be *nailed* on the cross, so that I may die to sin, and have a *new* life through your righteousness – 1 Pet. 2:24

- I thank you, Lord, for the books of *Numbers*, *Nehemiah*, and the book of *Nahum* that teach me your Word – Num.; Ne.; Na.
- Lord God, blessed be your glorious *name*, and may it be exalted – Neh. 9:5

Prayer Requests:

- Jesus, I pray that you will always keep me *next* to you – Ps. 73:28; Jam. 4:8
- Lord, I *need* you to stay *near* me 24/7 – Ps. 145:8; Ps. 65:4; Jer. 23:23
- Lord, I thank you because you know what I *need* before I ask – Phil. 4:19
- Lord, teach me to *number* my days, that I may gain a heart of wisdom – Ps. 90:12
- Father God, please lead me along the *narrow* way that leads to eternal life – Matt. 7:14
- Lord God, may the *nations* be glad and sing for joy, because You rule with equity and You guide the *nations* of the earth – Ps. 67:4

Prayer for the People in your Circle:

- I pray for my *neighbors* and my *neighborhood* to come together in love and for Your glory. I also pray for the *nurses* that tend to and minister to the sick throughout the world.
- I pray that *Noel* will know you, God, more intimately and glorify you in every area of his life (Pray for any specific needs you know about).
- I pray for *Natalie*, that she will know you, God, more intimately and glorify you in every area of her life (Pray for any specific needs you know about).

- I pray for *Nick*, so he will know you, God, more intimately and glorify you in every area of his life (Pray for any specific needs you know about).
- I pray for *Nancy*, that she will know you, God, more intimately and glorify you in every area of her life (Pray for any specific needs you know about).

N

Worship God because of who He is:

- _____
- _____
- _____
- _____
- _____
- _____
- _____
- _____
- _____
- _____
- _____
- _____
- _____
- _____

Praise God for what he has done:

- _____
- _____
- _____
- _____
- _____
- _____
- _____
- _____
- _____
- _____
- _____
- _____
- _____
- _____

Prayer Requests:

- _____
- _____
- _____
- _____
- _____
- _____
- _____
- _____
- _____
- _____

Prayer for the People in your Circle:

- _____
- _____
- _____
- _____
- _____
- _____
- _____
- _____
- _____
- _____

O

Worship God because of who He is:

- LORD GOD, you are the Alpha and *Omega* – Rev 22:13
- Father God/Jesus, you are number *one* in my life – Acts 4:12; Phil. 2:9
- Lord, you are *omnipotent* (with unlimited powers) – Matt. 19:26
- You are *omnipresent* (everywhere, at the same all times) – Ps. 139
- You are *omniscient* (the all-knowing God) – Matt. 10:29
- Jesus, you are the *offspring* of King David – Rev. 22:16
- Jesus, you are the *one* and *only* Begotten Son of God – John 1:18; 1 John 4:9
- LORD, you are the *on* Time God – Eccl. 3:1, 11-12
- JESUS, you are the source of eternal salvation for all who *obey* You – Heb. 5:9

Praise God for what he has done:

- John 17:21-23 tells me that I'm *one* with you, Christ Jesus – 1 Cor. 12:27
- I thank you for *offering* Yourself for my sins – Eph. 5:2; Heb. 9:28
- Jesus, please show me how to live an *obedient* life – John 14:23; Joshua 1:8
- Father God, I praise you because you have always kept your *oath* – Deut. 7:8; Ps. 15:4
- Lord, I thank you for the incredible *opportunities* you have given me – Gal. 6:10
- Father God, your love *overflows* for me – 1 Thess. 3:12; 1 Tim. 1:14
- Sovereign LORD, you have made the heavens and earth by your power and *outstretched* hands – Jer. 23:17

- I thank you, Lord, for the book *Obadiah* that teaches me your Word – Ob.
- Thank you for all the *opportunity* I have received through your grace – Eph. 2:7

Prayer Requests:

- Jesus, please show me how to live an *obedient* life – John 14:26; Lk. 12:12
- Jesus, help me to *overcome* my trials and temptations – 2 Pet. 2:9; Matt. 4:1-10
- Lord God, I desire an *outpouring* of the Holy Spirit in my life – Joel 2:28-29
- Father God, please anoint my head with your *oil* in the name of Jesus – Ps. 23:5
- Thank you, Lord, for *ordaining* me into your service – 2 Cor. 6:17
- Lord God, please give me a deep *obsession* for your Word – Ps. 119:97
- I pray for the *orphans* and the widows all *over* the world – Jam. 1:27
- Lord God, may I always *obtain* favor from You - Prov. 12:2
- Father God, please make my children like *olive* plants round around my table - Ps. 128:3
- Lord, I pray that you may give us an *open* door to preach the Word of Christ everywhere – Col. 4:3
- LORD, please work righteousness and justice for all the *oppressed* – Ps. 103:6; Ps.9:9
- Father God, fill me with joy and peace as the Holy Spirit *overflows* in my life – Rom. 15:13

Prayer for the People in your Circle:

- Lord Jesus, I pray for *overseers* of Your church. I pray for my *optometrist* (Eye Doctor), and for the *orderlies* that perform their tasks to the glory of God.

- I pray that *Otis* will know you, God, more intimately and glorify you in every area of his life (Pray for any specific needs you know about).
- I pray for *Olivia*, that she will know you, God, more intimately and glorify you in every area of her life (Pray for any specific needs you know about).
- I pray for *Olan*, so he will know you, God, more intimately and glorify you in every area of his life (Pray for any specific needs you know about).
- I pray for *Omega*, that she will know you, God, more intimately and glorify you in every area of her life (Pray for any specific needs you know about).

O

Worship God because of who He is:

- _____
- _____
- _____
- _____
- _____
- _____
- _____
- _____
- _____
- _____
- _____
- _____
- _____
- _____
- _____

Praise God for what he has done:

- _____
- _____
- _____
- _____
- _____
- _____
- _____
- _____
- _____
- _____
- _____
- _____
- _____
- _____
- _____

Prayer Requests:

- _____
- _____
- _____
- _____
- _____
- _____
- _____
- _____
- _____
- _____

Prayer for the People in your Circle:

- _____
- _____
- _____
- _____
- _____
- _____
- _____
- _____
- _____
- _____

P

Worship God because of who He is:

- Lord Jesus, you are the High *Priest* in the order of Melchizedek – Heb. 5:10; 7:17
- Jesus, you are the *Perfecter* of my faith – Heb. 12:2
- Lord Jesus, you are my *Prophet, Priest* and King forever – Isa. 9:6-7; Ps. 110:4
- Jesus, you along are *preeminence* – Col. 1:18; Heb. 1:4
- You are the Lord of *Peace* (Jehovah-Shalom) – Judg. 6:24
- You are the God of *Providence* – Ps. 103:19; Ps. 145:17
- You are the Lord who is *Present* (Jehovah-Shammah) – Ezek. 48:35
- Jesus, you are the *Passover* Lamb in Exodus – 1 Cor. 5:7; 1 Pet.1:19
- You are the Great *Physician* that heals my body – Ps. 103:3; Ps. 107:20
- Jesus, you are my *propitiation* (my atoning sacrifice) – 1 John 2:2
- You are the blessed and only *potentate*, the King of kings, and Lord of lords – 1 Tim. 6:15
- Father, you are the God that *provides* (Jehovah-Jireh) – Gen. 22:14
- Lord God, you the *Potter*, I am Your clay – Isa. 64:8
- Jesus, you are the *Prince* of *Peace* – Isa. 9:6
- Lord God, you are the *Perfect* Father – Ps. 68:5; 1 John 3:1

Praise God for what he has done:

- I will *proclaim* your goodness all the days of my life to the world – Ps. 145:6
- Lord, thank you for saving me from the *penalty* of sin – Rom. 3:20-31
- You have saved me from the *power* of sin – Col. 1:13
- And one day from the *presence* of sin – Rom. 8:30

- Lord, I'm *protected* by your love when my enemies are *persecuting* me – Ps. 129:2; Ps. 143:9
- Father God, thank you for *pursuing* me when I was not *pursuing* you – Ps. 23:6
- Lord God, you are *patient* with me – 2 Pet. 3:9
- You alone, O God, are *praiseworthy* – Ps. 145:4; Ps. 135:5
- Jesus, you give my life *purpose* – John 10:10; Rom. 8:28
- I *praise* you, Jesus, for your *passion* (his suffering during his trials and death) – Gal. 5:24
- Lord, thank you for *providence* against all opposition – 1 Cor. 16:9
- I thank you for the Bible because it is my *playbook* for life – Matt. 4:4
- I praise you because all of your *promises* are true – 2 Cor. 1:20; Ps. 119:50
- I thank you, Lord, for the books of *Psalm, Proverbs, Philippians, Philemon* and the two books of *Peter* that teach me your Word – Ps.; Prov.; Phil. Philem.; 1 & 2 Pet.
- Lord, your *parables* teaches me godly wisdom and doctrine – Matt.; Mark, Luke, John
- Lord, I praise you for the *plans* You have for my life – Jer. 29:11

Prayer Requests:

- Lord Jesus, teach me how to *pray* – Lk. 11:1
- Father God, give me the sincere "*Phileo*" love for all my brothers and sisters – John 21:16; 1 Sam. 18:1-3
- Lord, bless the *preacher* that *preaches* the gospel to the *poor* in spirit – Lk. 4:18; Mk. 16:15
- Give me a *passion* for your Word and *passion* for the lost souls in this world – Jam. 5:20; Rom. 9:2-3
- Lord God, *please* forgive me for the time I cause you *pain* – Rom. 8:22
- Lord, help me to *persevere* under the trials and temptations with your *perfect peace* – Isa. 26:3; Col. 3:15; Jam. 1:12
- Lord, let your *precious* Holy Spirit fill me – Ex. 31:3; John 16:13

- Father, *please* keep my *parents*, and help me be the *parent* you called me to be – Prov. 22:6; Ex. 20:12; Eph. 6:1
- Lord, *please* keep my heart from the sin of *pride* – Ps. 19:13; Jam. 4:10
- Jesus, *purify* me with hyssop, and make me clean – Ps. 51:7
- Lord God, help me to *practice* what I *preach* – Jam. 1:22; Matt. 7:24
- Father God, give me the *perseverance* to make it through the dark times – Gal. 6:9;
- Jesus, *please* help me to fulfill my *potential* in you – Eph. 3:20; Pro. 19:21
- Lord Jesus, let me be with you in *paradise* – John 17:20; Lk. 23:43
- O LORD! Let no man *prevail* over me, and all nations be judged before you – Ps. 9:19

Prayer for the People in your Circle:

- I pray for the *President* of the United States, that he would do Your Will! I pray for the *police* officers that you would *protect* them, and for the *postal* workers for the jobs they do.
- I pray for my *pastor*, and all your *preachers* around the world that *proclaim* your truth.
- I pray that *Phillip* will know you, God, more intimately and glorify you in every area of his life (Pray for any specific needs you know about).
- I pray for *Phyllis*, that she will know you, God, more intimately and glorify you in every area of her life (Pray for any specific needs you know about).
- I pray for *Perry*, so he will know you, God, more intimately and glorify you in every area of his life (Pray for any specific needs you know about).
- I pray for *Pamela*, that she will know you, God, more intimately and glorify you in every area of her life (Pray for any specific needs you know about).

P

Worship God because of who He is:

- _____
- _____
- _____
- _____
- _____
- _____
- _____
- _____
- _____
- _____
- _____
- _____
- _____
- _____

Praise God for what he has done:

- _____
- _____
- _____
- _____
- _____
- _____
- _____
- _____
- _____
- _____
- _____
- _____
- _____
- _____

Prayer Requests:

- _____
- _____
- _____
- _____
- _____
- _____
- _____
- _____
- _____
- _____

Prayer for the People in your Circle:

- _____
- _____
- _____
- _____
- _____
- _____
- _____
- _____
- _____
- _____

Q

Worship God because of who He is:

- Father God, there is no *quantity* (amount or limit) of love or power in You – John 3:16; Rom. 5:8
- Lord, no one can *question* your judgment – 1 Cor. 3:12-15; Rev. 20:11-15; Rom. 14:12
- Father God, you alone can make the mountains *quake*, and the hills melt – Nah 1:5
- Lord, you give drink to every beast of the field, and you *quench* my thirst – Ps. 104:11
- Lord, I know you will judge the *quick* and the dead, so have mercy on me – 1 Pet. 4:5

Praise God for what he has done:

- Thank you for the *quality* of life you have given me – Phil. 4:19;
- Lord God, your Word *quenches* my thirst and feeds my soul – John 4:14; 6:35
- Jesus, I praise you because you have never *quit* on me – Deut. 31:8; Matt. 28:20
- I praise you for being that threefold cord which is not *quickly* broken in my life – Eccl. 4:12
- God, even when we were dead in sins, you *quickened* us (made us alive) together with Christ – Eph 2:5

Prayer Request:

- Father God, please *quicken* (to become fast) your spirit in me – Rom. 8:11
- Father, in the *quiet* times, please lead me – Ps. 85:8

- Lord God, please bless me that my *quiver* may be full – Ps. 127:5
- Father God, help me to never speak evil of anyone, to avoid *quarreling*, to be gentle, and to show your perfect courtesy toward all people – Tit. 3:2

Prayer the People in your Circle:

- Father God, I pray for the *Queens* you have placed in my life: my mother, grandmothers, wife, aunts and all the church mothers.
- I pray that *Quinson* will know you, God, more intimately and glorify you in every area of his life (Pray for any specific needs you know about).
- I pray for *Quita*, that she will know you, God, more intimately and glorify you in every area of her life (Pray for any specific needs you know about).
- I pray for *Quincy*, so he will know you, God, more intimately and glorify you in every area of his life (Pray for any specific needs you know about).
- I pray for *Queen*, that she will know you, God, more intimately and glorify you in every area of her life (Pray for any specific needs you know about).

Q

Worship God because of who He is:

- _____
- _____
- _____
- _____
- _____
- _____
- _____
- _____
- _____
- _____
- _____
- _____
- _____
- _____

Praise God for what he has done:

- _____
- _____
- _____
- _____
- _____
- _____
- _____
- _____
- _____
- _____
- _____
- _____
- _____
- _____

Prayer Requests:

- _____
- _____
- _____
- _____
- _____
- _____
- _____
- _____
- _____
- _____

Prayer for the People in your Circle:

- _____
- _____
- _____
- _____
- _____
- _____
- _____
- _____
- _____
- _____

R

Worship God because of who He is:

- Lord God, you are Jehovah-*Rophe* (you're my healer) – Ex. 15:26
- Lord God, you are Jehovah-*Rohi* (you're my shepherd) – Ps. 23:1
- Father, you are the Lord, our *Righteousness* (Jehovah-Tsidkenu) – Jer. 23:6
- Lord Jesus, you are the *Righteous* King – Isa. 9:6
- Jesus, you are the *radiance* of God's Glory – Heb. 1:3
- You are the *Righteous* Branch – Jer. 23:5
- You alone are to be *revered* – Deut. 13:4; Ps. 89:7
- Lord Jesus, I give you all the *reverence* because you are my *redeemer* – Job 19:25; Ps. 19:14
- Lord, you are my *refuge* in times of trouble – Ps. 46
- Jesus, you are The *Root* of David – Rev. 5:5; Rev. 22:16
- You are my *Rock* that cannot be moved – 1 Cor. 10:4
- Father God, you are the only *reason* I exist – 1 Cor. 8:6
- Jesus, you are my Lord, *Ruler* and Savior of my life – Isa. 33:22
- Father God, all that you do is *remarkable* – Jer. 33:3
- Jesus, you are the *Rose* of Sharon – SS. 2:1
- Lord God, you are the God of unlimited *resources* – Gen. 18:14; Matt. 19:26
- Jesus, you are my *Rabbi*, my master and teacher – Matt. 23:8

Praise God for what he has done:

- Lord, I will *rejoice* and be glad, because great is my *reward* in heaven – Ps. 118:24
- I am the *righteousness* of you, God – 2 Cor. 5:21
- I am *redeemed* from the curse of the law – Gal. 3:13
- Lord God, I praise You for my washing of the *rebirth* and *renewal* by the Holy Spirit – Tit. 3:5

- I have been *reconciled* to you, God, through the blood of Jesus – 2 Cor. 5:18
- Through you, Jesus, I have been made me into a *Royal Priest* – 1 Pet. 2:9
- I thank you for my eternal *redemption* – Heb. 9:12
- Jesus, I thank you for the *reconciliation*; you have *reconciled* me back to the Father – 2 Cor. 5:18
- Jesus, your *resurrection* gave me victory over death and guarantees me eternal life – 1 Cor. 15:57; 1 John 5:4
- I praise you for *ransoming* me – 1 Tim. 2:6; Matt. 20:28
- Father God, you have *refined* me better than silver or gold, for your glory alone – Ps. 66:10; Isa. 48:10
- I know that you love me because you *rebuke* and discipline everyone you love – Rev. 3:19
- Jesus, you *rose* from the dead to give me victory over the grave – 1 Cor. 15:57
- Jesus, I love you, because you *respond* to my every need – Phil. 4:19
- I praise you because you give us *rain* in times of need – Zech. 10:1
- I thank you, Lord, for the book of *Ruth*, *Romans* and the book of *Revelation* that teach me your Word – Ruth; Rom.; Rev.
- Jesus, I praise you for the *relationship* I have with you – Rom. 5:10

Prayer Requests:

- Father God, I have sinned before you, and I *repent* now – Acts 3:19
- Jesus, *restore* the joy of your salvation . . . please! – Ps. 51:12
- Father God, I come to you to *rededicate* my life to you, today – Num. 6:12
- *Renew* a steadfast spirit within me – Ps. 51:10
- Help me show proper *respect* to everyone – Rom. 13:7
- Lord God Almighty, your Word said that I will *reign* with you – 2 Tim. 2:12
- Father God, make your *revelation* of your Word clear to me – Hab. 2:2

- Jesus, let me *reflect* your light in this world – Matt. 14:16
- Please help me to *recognize* the tricks of Satan – 2 Cor. 2:11; Eph. 6:11
- Jesus, please *record* my name in the Lamb's Book of Life – Rev. 3:5
- Father, help me to *represent* Your Son in all I do – 2 Cor. 5:20
- Lord Jesus, please *receive* my soul and spirit into Your kingdom – Rom. 8:9
- Lord Jesus, *remember* me . . . just *remember* me – Lk. 23:42; Jud. 16:28; Jer. 15:15; Ps. 106:4
- Lord, help us to *run* with patience the *race* that is set before us – Heb. 12:1
- Jesus, thank you for ministering, and for giving your life as a *ransom* for my sins – Matt. 20:28
- Psalms 126:5 states, "They that sow in tears shall *reap* in joy." Lord let me *reap* that harvest – Ps. 126:5
- Lord, please forgive me for the times I have *rebelled* against You in my heart – Lam. 1:18
- Lord, please plant me by the *rivers* of water, that I may be fruitful and prosper – Ps. 1:3

Prayer for the People in your Circle:

- Father God, I pray for the people that work in *rescue*, because they are an extension of your hand. I pray that you will keep the *railroad* engineers safe, and all that work on our *roads*.
- I pray that *Robert* will know you, God, more intimately and glorify you in every area of his life (Pray for any specific needs you know about).
- I pray for *Rhonda*, that she will know you, God, more intimately and glorify you in every area of her life (Pray for any specific needs you know about).
- I pray for *Ronnie*, so he will know you, God, more intimately and glorify you in every area of his life (Pray for any specific needs you know about).
- I pray for *Rosalind*, that she will know you, God, more intimately and glorify you in

R

Worship God because of who He is:

- _____
- _____
- _____
- _____
- _____
- _____
- _____
- _____
- _____
- _____
- _____
- _____
- _____
- _____
- _____

Praise God for what he has done:

- _____
- _____
- _____
- _____
- _____
- _____
- _____
- _____
- _____
- _____
- _____
- _____
- _____
- _____
- _____

Prayer Requests:

- _____
- _____
- _____
- _____
- _____
- _____
- _____
- _____
- _____
- _____

Prayer for the People in your Circle:

- _____
- _____
- _____
- _____
- _____
- _____
- _____
- _____
- _____
- _____

S

Worship God because of who He is:

- Lord God, you are Jehovah-*Shalom* (you're my peace) – Jud. 6:24
- Father God, you are Jehovah-*Shammah* (you're the Lord that is there) – Ezek. 48:35
- You are The LORD My *Sanctifier* (Jehovah-M'Kaddesh), who makes you holy – Lev. 20:7
- You are *Savior, Savior, Savior*! (saves, rescues, or delivers) – Eph. 5:23; Titus 1:4; 3:6; 2 Pet. 2:20
- *Sacred* is your Name, O Lord (JHVH – Jehovah) – Ex. 20:7
- Father, you are the *self-existent* One – Ex. 3:14
- You are the Great *Shepherd* that found me when I was lost – Lk. 15:3-7; 1 Pet. 2:25
- Jesus, you called yourself the *Son* of Man to relate with me – Mk. 8:31; Acts 7:56
- Jesus, you are the Anointed *Son* – Acts 10:38; Lk. 4:18
- Lord God, you are the leader of my *soul* – Ps. 62:5;
- Jesus, you are the *Seed* of David – Rom. 1:3; Jer. 23:5
- Lord, your *Shield* of Faith protects me from the attacks of the evil one – Eph. 6:16
- The *Sword* of the *Spirit*, which is your Word that guides me – Eph. 6:17; Heb. 4:12
- Jesus, you are my Lord and *Savior* – Rom. 10:9; Ps. 18:2
- You are the *sustainer* of my life – Ps. 54:4; Ruth 4:15
- You are the righteous *servant* that *saved* us – Isa. 53:11; Phil. 3:9
- Jesus, you are the *Son* of God – Mk. 1:11; Lk. 1:32
- Father God, you are the *source* that *supplies* all my needs – Phil. 4:19; Ps. 132:15
- You are our *sacrificed* Passover Lamb – 1 Cor. 5:7
- Jesus, you are the *source* of Eternal *Salvation* for all who obey You – Heb. 5:9
- Lord, you are the Rose of *Sharon* and the Lily of the valleys – Song of Sol. 2:1

Praise God for what he has done:

- Lord Jesus, I am dead to *sin* through your death on the cross – Rom, 6:2, 11; 1 Pet. 2:24
- Jesus, you are the *solution* to my needs, problems, and wants – Phil. 4:19; Ps. 23:1
- I have been raised up with you Christ Jesus, and I am *seated* in heavenly places – Eph. 4:6
- Lord, I will praise your Holy name everyday – whether it's the *Sabbath* day, *Saturday* or *Sunday* – Ps. 145:2
- Jesus, I thank you for *shedding* your blood for me – 1 John 1:7; Heb. 9:22
- Thank you for *sacrificing* everything for me – Heb. 9:28; 1 Cor. 15:3-4
- Lord, you have put my *sins* into the *sea* of Forgetfulness – Mic. 7:19
- Father God, your Holy *Scripture* is food to my *soul* – Jer. 15:16; Ps. 119:103;
- Jesus, thank you for providing my *sanctification* – Heb. 10:10; 1 Cor. 6:11
- Father God, I thank you for the eternal *security* I have in Jesus – Jude. 24
- I praise you because I'm *sealed* for the day of redemption – Eph. 4:30
- Jesus, I praise you for the *sovereignty* I have in you – Ps. 115:3; Rom. 8:28
- I praise you because your weapons are more *sophisticated* than this world has ever *seen* – 2 Cor. 10:4;
- I praise you because you have healed me when I was *sick* – Jer. 17:14; Ps. 30:2
- I praise you because you watch over me when I'm *sleeping* and keep me *safe* – Ps. 4:8
- Jesus, thank you that I'm invited to the Wedding *supper* of the Lamb – Isa. 25:6; Rev. 19:9
- Lord, your Word calls me a *Saint* – Rom. 1:7; 1 Cor. 1:2; Phil. 1:1
- Thank you, Lord, that for everything there is a *season*, and a purpose – Eccl. 3:1

- Father God, you have given me the best robe, put a ring on my hand, and *shoes* on my feet – Lk. 15:22
- Jesus, I thank you that nothing can *separate* me from your love – Rom. 8:37-39

Prayer Requests:

- Lord Jesus, let me hear Your voice *say* well done, My good and faithful *servant* – Matt. 25:21, 23;
- Lord, please give me *strength* when I am weak – Eph. 6:10; Isa. 40:29
- Holy *Spirit*, help me to *seek* and find the kingdom and its righteousness – Matt. 6:33; Luke 11:9
- *Sweet* Jesus, please remove any and every *stronghold* from my life – 1 Cor. 10:13; Eph. 6:13-18; 2 Cor. 10:3-4
- Jesus, pour out your *supernatural* power in abundance on me – 1 Tim. 1:14; Joel 2:28
- Lord God, *seal* me in your *Spirit* – Eph. 1:13; 2 Cor. 1:22; Eph. 4:30
- Lord Jesus, I pray that NO *sexual* immorality, *selfishness* or *slander* be attached to my name and bring your name *shame* – Eph. 5:3; Col. 3:5
- Help me be a person of *self*-control – Titus 1:8; 1 Tim. 3:2
- Father, help me to endure hardness, as a good *soldier* of Christ Jesus -2 Tim. 2:3
- Lord, I vow to be a good *steward* of the resources you have put under my care – 1 Pet. 4:10; 1 Cor. 4:1
- Lord Jesus, I *submit* to your Lordship and rule; I come in full *submission* – Jam. 4:7; Rom. 13:1-7; 1 Pet. 2:13-17; Jam. 4:7;
- Lord, make me a *sanctuary* of Your *Spirit*, and fill it with yourself – 1 Cor. 6:19; 1 Pet. 2:5
- Jesus, I pray that my life may be in order at your *Second* Coming – Rev. 1:7; John 14:1-3; 1 Thess. 4:16-17
- Lord I pray for *success* in all I do, that I might bring you glory – Matt. 5:16
- Father, continue to let me be *Salt* and Light for you in this dark world – Matt. 5:13-14
- *Search* me, O God, and know my heart – Ps. 139:23

- Lord, in times of trouble, hide me under the *shadow* of thy wings – Ps. 17:8, 63:7
- Lord, please purge me and wash me, and I will be whiter than *snow* – Ps. 51:7
- I thank you, Lord, for the book of *Samuel* and the book of *Song of Solomon* that teach me your Word – 1 & 2 Sam.; SOS.

Prayer for the People in your Circle:

- Father, God I pray for the *seasoned Saints* in my life. I pray for my *supervisors* in my workplace. I pray for all of the *students* that are under my care.
- I pray that *Scott* will know you, God, more intimately and glorify you in every area of his life (Pray for any specific needs you know about).
- I pray for *Sharon,* that *she* will know you, God, more intimately and glorify you in every area of her life (Pray for any specific needs you know about).
- I pray for *Samuel*, so he will know you, God, more intimately and glorify you in every area of his life (Pray for any specific needs you know about).
- I pray for *Sarah*, that *she* will know you God more intimately and glorify you in every area of her life (Pray for any specific needs you know about).

S

Worship God because of who He is:

- _____
- _____
- _____
- _____
- _____
- _____
- _____
- _____
- _____
- _____
- _____
- _____
- _____
- _____
- _____

Praise God for what he has done:

- _____
- _____
- _____
- _____
- _____
- _____
- _____
- _____
- _____
- _____
- _____
- _____
- _____
- _____
- _____

Prayer Requests:

- _____
- _____
- _____
- _____
- _____
- _____
- _____
- _____
- _____
- _____

Prayer for the People in your Circle:

- _____
- _____
- _____
- _____
- _____
- _____
- _____
- _____
- _____
- _____

T

Worship God because of who He is:

- Lord, you are Jehovah-*Tsidkenu* (you're my righteousness) – Jer. 23:6
- God, you are the source of all *truth* – 1 Cor. 8:6
- All Your Words are *trustworthy* – 2 Sam. 7:28
- Father God, you are my strong and high *tower* – Ps. 61:3
- Jesus, you are *the* way, *the Truth,* and life – John 14:6
- Father God, you are *the* Only God with His *throne* in heaven – Isa. 66:1
- Lord God, all of creation *testifies to* your existence – Rom. 1:20
- You are *The Triune* God; *The* God of *the Trinity* – Gen. 1:26
- Jesus, you are the *True* Vine – John 15:1
- Lord God, you are *transcendent* (in you all *things* hold *together*) – Col. 6:17
- LORD, you are in your Holy *Temple*; You sit upon *the Throne* of holiness - Ps. 11:4; Ps. 47:8

Praise God for what he has done:

- *Through* you, Jesus, I am *the Temple* of the Holy Spirit – 1 Cor. 6:19
- *Thank* you, Jesus, for *teaching* me your righteousness – Ps. 25:5
- Lord, I praise you because I have a right to *The Tree* of Life – Rev. 22:14
- Lord God, I give you all my *tribute* in praise and worship daily – Ps. 83:12
- Jesus, I praise you because you are *the* Greatest *treasure* anyone could have – Lk. 12:34
- Father, I *thank* you for *the talents* and gifts you have given your servant – 1 Pet. 4:10
- Lord, I come before you with *thanksgiving* in my heart for all you have done – Ps. 100:4

93

- Lord Jesus, you are the same yesterday, *today, tomorrow* and forever – Heb. 13:8
- I *thank* you, Jesus, for *transforming* my sinful life by your *truth* – Titus 3:5
- Jesus, you have prepared your *table* for me – Ps. 23:5
- I praise you for your *traveling* mercies – Ps. 23:4
- I love you because of your *tenderness towards* me – 2 Cor. 1:3
- *Thank* you, Jesus, for always *taking time* out for me – Ps. 121:4
- Lord, I *thank* you for your *Torah*, your Pentateuch, your Word (the first five books of the Bible) – Gen.; Ex.; Lev.; Num.; Deut.
- I thank you, Lord, for the book of *Titus* and the *two* books of *Timothy* and the *two* books of *Thessalonians* that *teach* me your Word – Titus; 1 & 2 Tim.; Thess.

Prayer Requests:

- Father God, blot out all my *transgressions* – Isa. 43:25
- Lord God, please keep my *testimony* from slander – 1 Pet. 2:12
- Lord, help me to persevere under the *trials* and *temptations* through your perfect peace – Jam. 1:2-18
- Lord, make me your living *Tabernacle* for your glory – 1 Cor. 3:16
- Jesus, keep my *tongue* in check, and let me speak only your *truth* and blessing – Jam. 3:2
- Father God, help me *to* be faithful in my *tithe* – Mal. 3:8
- God, help me to use *the time* you have given wisely – Eccl: 3:2-8; Eph. 5:16
- Lord God, please, *touch the* hearts of *the* unbelievers in my family – John 6:44
- Lord, give me your living water, so that I may not *thirst* – John 4:14
- *teach* me *to* do your will, Lord – Ps. 143:10

Prayer for the People in your Circle:

- Father God, I pray for my *teacher* of *the truth* in your Word. I pray for *the therapists* that counsel your people, and *the* people *that* work in *technology* displaying your wisdom.
- I pray that *Tony* will know you, God, more intimately and glorify you in every area of his life (Pray for any specific needs you know about).
- I pray for *Terri*, that she will know you, God, more intimately and glorify you in every area of her life (Pray for any specific needs you know about).
- I pray for *Thomas*, so he will know you, God, more intimately and glorify you in every area of his life (Pray for any specific needs you know about).
- I pray for *Tracy*, that she will know you God more intimately and glorify you in every area of her life (Pray for any specific needs you know about).

T

Worship God because of who He is:

- _____
- _____
- _____
- _____
- _____
- _____
- _____
- _____
- _____
- _____
- _____
- _____
- _____
- _____

Praise God for what he has done:

- _____
- _____
- _____
- _____
- _____
- _____
- _____
- _____
- _____
- _____
- _____
- _____
- _____
- _____

Prayer Requests:

- _____
- _____
- _____
- _____
- _____
- _____
- _____
- _____
- _____
- _____

Prayer for the People in your Circle:

- _____
- _____
- _____
- _____
- _____
- _____
- _____
- _____
- _____
- _____

U

Worship God because of who He is:

- Lord God, you alone created the *universe* — Gen. 1:1
- Father God, you are *unchanging*: the same, yesterday, today and forever — Heb. 13:8
- Lord God, it is you, and you alone that *uphold* me – Ps. 16:5
- Father God, you alone *understand* what I'm going through – Deut. 31:6
- Jesus, you are the *unblemished* Lamb – 1 Pet. 1:19
- Lord Jesus, your love for me is *unconditional* – Rom. 5:8
- Father God, to grasp all of you is *unimaginable* – Eph. 3:18
- Jesus, you made me *unique* and for your glory – Ps. 139:13

Praise God for what he has done:

- Lord, I thank you for the times you *used* me as your instrument – John 15:16
- Jesus, you are *understanding* and forgiving – Ps. 111:10
- Lord God, you picked me *up* out of muck-and-mire clay – Ps. 40:2
- Jesus Christ, you alone are my *ultimate* life changer – Ps. 51:10
- Jesus, I am *unworthy* of your love; but you *understand* me – Gen. 32:10
- Jesus, you are able to save *us* to the *uttermost*, everyone that comes to you – Heb. 7:25
- Lord, help me to be steadfast, *unmovable*, and always abounding in your works – 1 Cor. 15:58

Prayer Requests:

- Lord, teach me to walk *upright* before you – Ps. 25:4
- Jesus, I pray for *unity* in the body (church) – Eph. 4:3
- Lord Jesus, please keep me from becoming *unfruitful* and *ungodly* – Eph. 5:11

- Father God, help your servant to be faithful and never be in *unbelief* – Ps. 86:2
- Jesus, I pray for my *uncles* – 1 Tim. 2:1
- Father God, may I never take counsel of the *ungodly*, sinners, nor from the scornful – Ps. 1:1
- Lord, I am a person of *unclean* lips, please clean my heart – Isa. 6:5
- Lord God, may I never be destroyed because I'm *unfaithful* to you – Ps. 73:27
- Jesus, may nothing be found *undone* of all that you have commanded of me – Josh. 11:15
- Teach me, O LORD, how-to walk-in truth; and *unite* my heart to you in holy reverence – Ps. 86:11

Prayer for the People in your Circle:

- Lord, I pray that you will touch the hearts of all the *unbelievers* I know. I pray for the *umpires* and officials that keep our games in order. I pray for the *ushers* that serve and assist us.
- I pray that *Ulysses* will know you, God, more intimately and glorify you in every area of his life (Pray for any specific needs you know about).
- I pray for *Uriah*, that she will know you, God, more intimately and glorify you in every area of her life (Pray for any specific needs you know about).
- I pray for *Usain*, so he will know you, God, more intimately and glorify you in every area of his life (Pray for any specific needs you know about).
- I pray for *Ursula*, that she will know you God more intimately and glorify you in every area of her life (Pray for any specific needs you know about).

U

Worship God because of who He is:

- _____
- _____
- _____
- _____
- _____
- _____
- _____
- _____
- _____
- _____
- _____
- _____
- _____
- _____

Praise God for what he has done:

- _____
- _____
- _____
- _____
- _____
- _____
- _____
- _____
- _____
- _____
- _____
- _____
- _____
- _____

Prayer Requests:

- _____
- _____
- _____
- _____
- _____
- _____
- _____
- _____
- _____
- _____

Prayer for the People in your Circle:

- _____
- _____
- _____
- _____
- _____
- _____
- _____
- _____
- _____
- _____

V

Worship God because of who He is:

- Jesus, you are the chosen, and most *valuable* stone in the building of God – Ps.118:22
- Father, I love you because you always keep your *vows* – Heb.13:8
- Jesus, you are my *valiant* warrior; you are fearless and courageous – Ex.15:3
- Jesus, you are the living true *vine* that supplies me – John 15:1-4
- Lord Jesus, the Holy Spirit *verifies* your Word – 1 Cor. 12:3

Praise God for what he has done:

- Your Word tells me I am *victorious* in you, Christ Jesus – Rev. 21:7
- Thank you, Jesus, for allowing me to hear your *voice* – John 10:27
- Thank you, Jesus, for *vindicating* me by your blood – Ps. 35:24
- Father God, help me keep my *vows* to you – Eccl. 5:4-8
- I praise you because you *volunteered* to die for me – John 10:18
- Thank you for the *visitation* of your Spirit, Jesus – Isa. 11:2
- I praise you because you have removed the *veil* – 2 Cor. 3:16
- Lord, I praise you because you *value* me more than the sparrows – Luke 12:7
- I thank you, God, for the *victory* through your son Jesus – 1 Cor. 15:57

Prayer Request:

- Hear my *voice* when I call, O Lord, and answer me – Ps. 27:7
- Lord Jesus, I pray that you would use me as your *vessel* – 2 Tim. 2:21

- Lord, please keep my wife (or self) a *virtuous* woman (or person) – Prov. 31:10-31
- Jesus, keep my *vision* focused on you – Ps. 16:8
- God, your Word is so *valuable* to my growth – 2 Tim. 3:16-17
- Father God, please keep my spouse (relationships) and me (?) from becoming *vulnerable* – 1 Thess. 5:13
- Lord, may I never live-in *violation* to your Word – Deut. 4:2
- Jesus, let me *view* people through your eyes – Ps. 119:18
- Lord, when I walk through the *Valley* of the Shadow of Death, you are with me – Ps. 23:4
- Lord, please show me your *vision*, that I may not perish – Prov. 29:18
- *Visit* me, O LORD, with your salvation – Ps. 106:4

Prayer the People in your Circle:

- Father God, I pray for all the *victims* of natural disasters. I pray for all the *veterans*, that you will meet their needs. Also, I pray for the *violinist* that play praise music to your glory.
- I pray that *Victor* will know you, God, more intimately and glorify you in every area of his life (Pray for any specific needs you know about).
- I pray for *Virginia*, that she will know you, God, more intimately and glorify you in every area of her life (Pray for any specific needs you know about).
- I pray for *Vincent*, so he will know you, God, more intimately and glorify you in every area of his life (Pray for any specific needs you know about).
- I pray for *Vickie*, that she will know you, God, more intimately and glorify you in every area of her life (Pray for any specific needs you know about).

V

Worship God because of who He is:

- _____
- _____
- _____
- _____
- _____
- _____
- _____
- _____
- _____
- _____
- _____
- _____
- _____
- _____

Praise God for what he has done:

- _____
- _____
- _____
- _____
- _____
- _____
- _____
- _____
- _____
- _____
- _____
- _____
- _____
- _____

Prayer Requests:

- _____
- _____
- _____
- _____
- _____
- _____
- _____
- _____
- _____
- _____

Prayer for the People in your Circle:

- _____
- _____
- _____
- _____
- _____
- _____
- _____
- _____
- _____
- _____

W

Worship God because of who He is:

- You are *worthy*, O Lord, to receive glory and honor power and praise – Rev. 4:11
- I *will worship* you all the days of my life – Ps. 66:4
- Lord God, you are the *warrior* that fights all my battles – Isa.49:25; Ps. 118:6
- Father God, you are the true *wise* God, and all *wisdom* come from you – Pro. 2:6
- Jesus, you are The *Way*, the truth, and life – John 14:6
- You are the *Wonderful* Counselor – Isa. 9:6
- Jesus, you are the Living *Word* – John 1:1

Praise God for what he has done:

- **I am Forgiven** of all my sins and *washed* in your blood, Jesus – 1 John 1:7
- You, Jesus, have brought me out of darkness into your *wonderful* light – 1 Pet. 2:9
- I praise you because you have removed every *weight* and sin that beset me – Heb. 12:1
- Lord, if it's your *will*, may I see tomorrow – Ps. 143:10
- I thank you for forgiving me for all the *wickedness* I have committed – 1 John 1:9
- I Praise you, Lord, for the Spiritual *weapons* you have given me – 2 Cor. 10:4
- Thank you, Jesus, for saving me from your *wrath* of God – Rom. 9:5
- I praise you because You have given us your Holy *Word* – Ps. 191:105
- All your *works* praise You, LORD; I *will* faithfully exult in You – Ps. 145:10
- Lord, I rejoice because my name is *written* in the Lamb's Book of Life in heaven – Lk. 10:20

- I thank you, Lord, that I am invited to the "*Wedding* Feast of the Lamb" – Rev. 19:6-9
- Lord, your *Word* tells me to *wait* on you; to be of good courage, and you *will* strengthen my heart – Ps. 27:14
- Lord Christ, I praise you for paying the *wages* of sin for me, and for the gift of God *which* is eternal life – Rom. 6:23

Prayer Requests:

- Jesus, please *wash* away all my iniquities – Ps. 51:2
- Lord, please *walk with* me – 2 John 1:6
- Help me serve others *wholeheartedly, with* Agape love – 1 Cor. 13:1-13
- Father God, if it's your *will*, please *widen* my territory – 1 Chr. 4:10
- Lord, please continue to bless my *wife* and kids – 2 Tim. 4:22
- Lord God, please give me *wisdom* and understanding – Ps. 111:10
- Lord, *when war* breaks out against me, I will be comforted – Ps. 27:3
- Lord, help me to seek you *with* my heart and never *wander* away from your commandments – Ps. 119:10
- Lord, never let me become arrogant, nor to put my hope in *wealth* – 1 Tim. 6:17
- Jesus, please lead me to the spring of living *water* – Rev. 7:17
- Have mercy upon me, O LORD, for I am *weak*; strengthen and make me strong – Ps. 6:2
- Lord, please don't let Satan sift me as *wheat* – Lk. 22:31
- Lord, *watch* over my *ways*, and keep me on the path of righteousness – Ps. 1:6
- Lord, let me bow before your throne, clothed *with* a *white* robe, and palms in my hands – Rev. 7:9
- Lord God, please protect me today as I go out among the *wolves* of this *world* – Lk. 10:3

Prayer for the People in your Circle:

- Father God, I pray that you would comfort the *widows* and the *widowers* all over the *world*. I pray for the protection of the *welders* and the *wardens*.
- I pray that *William* will know you, God, more intimately and glorify you in every area of his life (Pray for any specific needs you know about).
- I pray for *Wanda*, that she will know you, God, more intimately and glorify you in every area of her life (Pray for any specific needs you know about).
- I pray for *Willie*, so he will know you, God, more intimately and glorify you in every area of his life (Pray for any specific needs you know about).
- I pray for *Windy*, that she will know you, God, more intimately and glorify you in every area of her life (Pray for any specific needs you know about).

W

Worship God because of who He is:

- _____
- _____
- _____
- _____
- _____
- _____
- _____
- _____
- _____
- _____
- _____
- _____
- _____
- _____
- _____

Praise God for what he has done:

- _____
- _____
- _____
- _____
- _____
- _____
- _____
- _____
- _____
- _____
- _____
- _____
- _____
- _____
- _____

Prayer Requests:

- _____
- _____
- _____
- _____
- _____
- _____
- _____
- _____
- _____
- _____

Prayer for the People in your Circle:

- _____
- _____
- _____
- _____
- _____
- _____
- _____
- _____
- _____
- _____

X

Worship God because of who He is:

- Father God, you are *Xavier* (means "bright; splendid; new house"): You are Bright, brighter that any light man can make. You are my dwelling place – John 14:2-3.
- Lord, you are sweeter the *Xylose* (a type of sugar) – 1 Pet. 2:3
-
-
-
-
-
-

Praise God for what he has done:

- Lord God, I will praise you with the *xylophone* – Ps. 150:3-5
-
-
-
-
-

Prayer Requests:

- Lord God, may I never be a *Xenophobe* (a person who fears or hates foreigners, people from different cultures, or strangers). Help me love people with your love – Lev. 19:33-34; Heb. 13:2; 1 John 4:18-21
- Jesus, please cleanse everyone I know with *Xanthoma* (skin disease) – Ps. 51:2; Matt. 10:8
- Lord, keep my eye, mind and heart from everything *X-Rated* - Job 31:1
- Father God give us the *Xenophilia* (love of foreigners) to fulfill your command in Matt. 28:19-20. – 1 Pet. 2:17; Philem. 1:5-7

- Lord, help me show Your love to every *Xanthippe* person (ill-tempered woman) – Lk. 6:35
-

Prayer for the People in your Circle:

- Father God I pray for the *xylophone* players that play praise music to your glory.
- I pray that *Xavier* will know you, God, more intimately and glorify you in every area of his life (Pray for any specific needs you know about).
- I pray for *Xanthus*, that she will know you, God, more intimately and glorify you in every area of her life (Pray for any specific needs you know about).
- I pray for *Xenia*, so he will know you, God, more intimately and glorify you in every area of his life (Pray for any specific needs you know about).
- I pray for *Xenophon*, that she will know you, God, more intimately and glorify you in every area of her life (Pray for any specific needs you know about).

X

Worship God because of who He is:

- _____
- _____
- _____
- _____
- _____
- _____
- _____
- _____
- _____
- _____
- _____
- _____
- _____
- _____
- _____

Praise God for what he has done:

- _____
- _____
- _____
- _____
- _____
- _____
- _____
- _____
- _____
- _____
- _____
- _____
- _____
- _____
- _____

Prayer Requests:

- _____
- _____
- _____
- _____
- _____
- _____
- _____
- _____
- _____
- _____

Prayer for the People in your Circle:

- _____
- _____
- _____
- _____
- _____
- _____
- _____
- _____
- _____
- _____

Y

Worship God because of who He is:

- *You* are (*YHWH*) *Yahweh*, the only God – Josh. 22:22
- I completely *yield* myself to *you*, Lord Jesus – Rom. 6:13
- *Your* will is now my will and *your* plans are my plans – 1 Thess. 5:18
- *You* are THE CHRIST JESUS – Mark 8:29
- Father God, *you* have proven *Yourself* faithful – Ps. 18:25
-

Praise God for what he has done:

- Lord, it's *You*, against *You* alone have I sinned and did evil in *Your* sight – Ps. 51:4
- I praise *You*, Lord, for the *years You* have let me live – Prov. 3:2
- Thank you for all the blessings I received *yesterday* – Deut. 28:8; Heb. 13:8
- Jesus, *you* have removed the *yoke* of sin from around my neck – Nah. 1:13
- Lord, may we praise *You* throughout the *yuletide* season (the Christmas season - period extending from Dec. 24 to Jan. 6) – Matt. 2:1-2; Isa. 9:6

Prayer Requests:

- Lord Jesus, I pray for the *youth* under my care – Ps. 119:9
- Help me to be on my guard against the *yeast* of the false teachers – Matt. 16:6
- Father God, may I always be about your work and never a *yenta* (gossip or busybody) – Prov. 20:19; 11:13
- Lord Jesus, please let my *yes* (*yea*) be *yes* (*yea*) and my no be no – Matt. 5:37
- Though I am free from all men, *Yet* I made myself a servant – 1 Cor. 9:19

115

- Lord, make me a good tree so I can *yield* good fruit for the kingdom – Matt 7:17
- Holy Spirit, do not let me be *yoked* together with an unbeliever – 2 Cor. 6:14
- Lord, please help me to flee from *youthful* lusts and pursue righteousness, faith, love and peace – 2 Tim. 2:22

Prayer for the People in your Circle:

- Father God, I pray for all the *young* people I work with.
- I pray that *Yancy* will know you, God, more intimately and glorify you in every area of his life (Pray for any specific needs you know about).
- I pray for *Yolanda*, that she will know you, God, more intimately and glorify you in every area of her life (Pray for any specific needs you know about).
- I pray for *Yowl*, so he will know you, God, more intimately and glorify you in every area of his life (Pray for any specific needs you know about).
- I pray for *Yvonne*, that she will know you, God, more intimately and glorify you in every area of her life (Pray for any specific needs you know about).

Y

Worship God because of who He is:

- _____
- _____
- _____
- _____
- _____
- _____
- _____
- _____
- _____
- _____
- _____
- _____
- _____

Praise God for what he has done:

- _____
- _____
- _____
- _____
- _____
- _____
- _____
- _____
- _____
- _____
- _____
- _____
- _____

Prayer Requests:

- _____
- _____
- _____
- _____
- _____
- _____
- _____
- _____
- _____
- _____

Prayer for the People in your Circle:

- _____
- _____
- _____
- _____
- _____
- _____
- _____
- _____
- _____
- _____

Z

Worship God because of who He is:

- Jesus, you are the stone in *Zion* – 1 Pet. 2:6
- Lord God you are *Zealous*; You are passionate in Your love of me – Tit. 2:14
-
-
-
-

Praise God for what he has done:

- I praise you
-
-
-
-
- I thank you, Lord, for the book of *Zephaniah*, and the book of *Zechariah* that teach me your Word – Zep.; Zech.

Prayer Requests:

- Lord Jesus, never let me lack *zeal* for you, your Word and service – Rom. 12:11
- Father God, let there be *zero* amount of sin within me – 2 Tim 2:14
- Lord God, please fill us with the Holy as you filled *Zacharias* - LK. 1:67
-
-
-

Prayer for the People in your Circle:

- Father God, I pray for *zoo-keepers*, that the animals will not harm them, and for the *Zoologists* that take care of the animals.
- I pray that *Zi'mere* will know you, God, more intimately and glorify you in every area of his life (Pray for any specific needs you know about).
- I pray for *Zelma*, that she will know you, God, more intimately and glorify you in every area of her life (Pray for any specific needs you know about).
- I pray for *Zaylin*, so he will know you, God, more intimately and glorify you in every area of his life (Pray for any specific needs you know about).
- I pray for *Zena*, that she will know you, God, more intimately and glorify you in every area of her life (Pray for any specific needs you know about).

Z

Worship God because of who He is:

- _____
- _____
- _____
- _____
- _____
- _____
- _____
- _____
- _____
- _____
- _____
- _____
- _____
- _____

Praise God for what he has done:

- _____
- _____
- _____
- _____
- _____
- _____
- _____
- _____
- _____
- _____
- _____
- _____
- _____
- _____

Prayer Requests:

- _____
- _____
- _____
- _____
- _____
- _____
- _____
- _____
- _____
- _____

Prayer for the People in your Circle:

- _____
- _____
- _____
- _____
- _____
- _____
- _____
- _____
- _____
- _____

The Conclusion

Understand that Prayer is a continuous adventure in drawing us closer to God/Jesus, and prayer helps us to develop our relationship with Him. Prayer involves the desire to hear His voice, to know His will, and to serve Him. Learning these basic skills will help us to communicate with God/Jesus in Spirit and Truth. With this understanding, we will have our prayers answered and receive more victories in our lives.

God has equipped us with many tools, gifts and talents, but none compare to the ability of approaching Him in prayer. When used properly, prayer is not only our most important tool or weapon, it can also be our best asset. We are told to Seek ye first the kingdom of God, and his righteousness; and all these things shall be added unto you (Matthew 6:33 NIV).

Take some time every day and pray your own alphabet prayer. He will hear you and answer you with His love, mercy and grace.

I pray that you didn't fall asleep or lose focus; and we hope you enjoyed your time praying through the letters of the alphabet. To God be the glory – AMEN!

For other helpful materials contact us at:

The Matthew 28:20 Group, LLC
P.O. Box 3613
Rock Hill, S.C. 29732

Web Site: Matthew2820group.com

Printed in the United States
by Baker & Taylor Publisher Services